Canadian Receipt Book

Containing Over 500 Valuable Receipts for the Farmer and the Housewife

First Published in 1867

**Preface by Melissa McAfee
Edited by Jen Rubio**

Rock's Mills Press
Oakville, Ontario
2018

640
CAN

Published by
ROCK'S MILLS PRESS

www.rocksmillspress.com

Copyright © 2018 by Rock's Mills Press
Preface copyright © 2018 by Melissa McAfee

Original edition first published in 1867

978-1-77244-124-6 (paperback, Canada and US)
978-1-77244-119-2 (paperback, international)
978-1-77244-114-7 (paperback, Amazon)
978-1-77244-115-5 (casebound)

For information, contact:
Customer Service
Rock's Mills Press
2645 Castle Hill Crescent
Oakville, ON L6H 6J1
customer.service@rocksmillspress.com

Contents

Preface by Melissa McAfee / i

The Canadian Receipt Book; Containing Over 500 Valuable Receipts for the Farmer and the Housewife / 7

∼

Index / 198

Preface
by Melissa McAfee

Published in 1867, the year of Canadian Confederation, *The Canadian Receipt Book; Containing over 500 Valuable Receipts for the Farmer and the Housewife* is a fascinating glimpse into everyday life in Canada fifteen decades ago.

"Receipt" is an older term that refers to both cooking instructions as well as medicinal preparations, reminding us that in a mainly agrarian society of 1867, many Canadians were their own doctors, cooks, cleaners, farmers, veterinarians, beekeepers, and rat catchers. The title advertises 500 receipts, but in fact contains only 341. However, those 341 receipts cover an impressive range of topics. There are chapters on "Puddings," "Vegetables," "Observations for Making and Baking Cakes," "Home Brewery & Wines," "Receipts for Dyeing," "Toilet Receipts," and "Hints to Housekeepers." In addition to these household receipts, there is also advice for farmers on cattle, sheep, horses, pigs, and poultry, not to mention an entire section devoted to beekeeping.

Catherine Parr Traill, author of the popular *The Female Emigrant's Guide and Hints on Canadian Housekeeping* (Toronto, 1855), described Canada as "the land of cakes." However, here we have only 15 recipes for cakes; *The Canadian Receipt Book* is mostly concerned with the staples of food preparation and preservation, containing only a handful of sweet, dessert-like recipes such as "snow-balls" and orange fool. This focus on the utilitarian is introduced in the cookbook's preface: "In selecting the Recipes for this work, care has been taken to make sure of those only which can be relied on, and which are like to prove of practical use in the Canadian Country House."

Like many other cookbooks of the time, the recipes for food do not

~Preface by Melissa McAfee~

contain a list of ingredients, an ordered list of instructions to prepare the dish, standardized measurement, illustrations, or the yield of the dish (that is, the number of people who can be served). It would have been presumed that a competent householder would know how to execute the receipt. Many of the receipts appear to be of British origin, such as the recipes for fool, flummery, Welsh rabbit, plum cakes, and tea cakes. Although the author or source of the recipes cannot be easily determined, the evident emphasis on British cookery is in keeping with earlier English language Canadian cookbooks, which were often based on either British or American sources. There were also a handful of French recipes published in cookbooks in Quebec prior to Confederation; however, although Quebec had its own flourishing cuisine by 1867, there seems to be no effort to include receipts from that province. Some of the receipts may have been reprinted from the almanacs produced by the *Ottawa Citizen*, the publisher of the cookbook. Ontario was slow to embrace French cuisine: one of the earliest books to include a variety of ethnic recipes, *Cooking With an Accent* by Helen Gougeon, an Ottawa food journalist, was not published until nearly 80 years after Confederation.

There is a wide range of ales and wines available to Canadians now, but our ancestors of 150 years ago were clearly willing to make their own wine from whatever was available. In a world where the remedies for serious ailments included "blood and liver syrup" purchased "cheap and reliable" from chemists (who were also selling tobacco, hair dyes, and veterinary medicines), perhaps the occasional glass of home-made raspberry wine was as healthy as the next thing.

The cookbook also contains 106 advertisements, a large number for a cookbook. These appear throughout the book on almost every right-hand page, reflecting a surprising range of businesses operating in downtown Ottawa in the year of Canadian Confederation. The advertisements are fascinating in their diversity, including insurance companies, dry goods, hardware stores, shoes, pharmacies, tea and coffee, photography, watches and jewelers, fire proof safes, grocers, printers, and hotels. In addition to an impressive range of wines, spirits, brandies, imported ales, tobacco, and saloons, we also see companies that offered several products or services at once: H.A. Palmer offering hairdressing, toys, and tobacco; Dr. J. Garvey's drug warehouse offering "Canadian" hair dye, "batchelor's" hair dye, and "cocoaine." (In the years before the the Opium and Narcotic Drug Act of 1929, cocaine was widely available, used in a range of different applications. On page 143 here, for example, a "surgeon dentist" offers "teeth extracted without pain" using an "ethereal spray." We can only speculate about the contents of what might have been used to concoct an "ethereal" spray; there were no labelling standards in 1867.)

Although there are no recipes for "Confederation cakes or puddings," two businessmen refer to Confederation: James Higginson advertises "The New Dominion Dry Goods & Ready Made Clothing" (81) and an ad for Thomas Dowsley's liquors states that his products are available "for sale by all the leading grocers and hotels in the New Dominion" (181). To most readers in 1867, celebrating the the new geoilitical landscape may well have taken a back seat to the complex problems of everyday survival.

As we celebrate 150 years of Canadian Confederation, this volume provides contemporary and unique insights into life in rural Canada in its first year as a Dominion. Life in the middle of the nineteenth century required a range of skills, from dealing with lice on chickens, to "stupefying bees with chloroform," to preserving watermelon. Our cookbooks have changed significantly over the years and reflect a less daunting domestic universe. Same country, different aspirations: nowadays we expect lifestyle cookbooks with sumptuous photography and calorie counts, often written by celebrity chefs, rather than tips for removing worms from a cow's bronchial tubes.

THE

CANADIAN RECEIPT BOOK;

CONTAINING OVER

500 VALUABLE RECEIPTS

FOR THE FARMER

AND

THE HOUSEWIFE.

Ottawa:
PRINTED FOR THE COMPILER AT "THE OTTAWA CITIZEN"
1867.

Pennock's Insurance Agency

J. T. & W. PENNOCK,

Agents for the following first-class British and American FIRE, LIFE and ACCIDENT INSURANCE COMPANIES:

FIRE.

ÆTNA INSURANCE COMPANY, of Hartford. Chartered A.D. 1819. Capital, $3,000,000; Assets, $4,650,938; Losses paid in 48 years, $21,371,972.

LIFE.

LIFE ASSOCIATION OF SCOTLAND. Founded 1838.
ANNUAL INCOME EXCEEDS . . $1,000,000
RESERVE FUND 5,000,000

ACCIDENT.

TRAVELLERS' INSURANCE COMPANY, of Hartford, issues all kinds of Accident and Life Policies.

EXCHANGE.

American Money, Greenbacks, Gold, Silver and Drafts bought and sold constantly, at closest rates.

PARLIAMENTARY AGENCY

Business transacted with all the Government Departments at Ottawa; Patents procured for Inventions, &c.

MINING CLAIMS.

Parties having Mining Claims to dispose of, or desiring to purchase, should call on us.

THE CANADIAN RECEIPT BOOK.

In selecting the Recipes for this work, care has been taken to make use of those only which can be relied on, and which are likely to prove of practical use in the Canadian Country House. The very best authorities on the various subjects have been consulted in compiling, so that perfect confidence may be placed in them. No pains has been spared to make this work a compendium of simple and useful Recipes.

THE RECEIPT BOOK.   [1867

DOMESTIC COOKERY.

PUDDINGS, &c.—The outside of a boiled pudding often tastes disagreeably; which arises from the cloth not being nicely washed, and kept in a dry place. It should be dipped in boiling water, squeezed dry, and floured when to be used. If bread, it should be tied loose; if batter, tight over. The water should boil quick when the pudding is put in; and it should be moved about for a minute, lest the ingredients should not mix. Batter-pudding should be strained through a coarse sieve, when all is mixed. In others the eggs separately. The pans and basins must be always buttered. A pan of cold water should be ready, and the pudding dipt in as soon as it comes out of the pot, and then it will not adhere to the cloth.

BREAD AND BUTTER PUDDING.—Slice bread spread with butter, and lay it in a dish with currents between each layer; and sliced citron, orange or lemon, if to be very nice. Pour over an unboiled custard of milk, two or three eggs, a few pimentos, and a very little ratafia, two hours at least before it is to be baked; and lade it over to soak the bread. A paste round the edge makes all puddings look better, but is not necessary.

A DUTCH RICE PUDDING.—Soak four ounces of rice warm water half an hour; drain the latter from it, throw it into a stew-pan, with half a pint of milk, ha stick of cinnamon, and simmer till tender. When c add four whole eggs well beaten, two ounces of bu melted in a tea-cupful of cream; and put three oun of sugar, a quarter of a nutmeg, and a good piece lemon peel. Put a light puff-paste into a mo dish, or grated tops and bottoms, and bake in oven.

GRANT & HENDERSON,

IMPORTERS OF

DRY GOODS, MILLINERY, MANTLES,

SILKS, SHAWLS, CLOTHS, CARPETS,

OIL CLOTHS, HOUSE FURNISHINGS, TRIMMINGS

&c., &c., &c.

ESTABLISHMENTS:

Robert's New Block, No. 20, Rideau Street, and the Bishop's Building, near the Cathedral, Sussex st.

AN EXCELLENT LEMON PUDDING.—Beat the yolks of four eggs; add four ounces of white sugar, the rind of a lemon being rubbed with some lumps of it to take the essence; then peel, and beat it in a mortar with the juice of a large lemon, and mixed all with four or five ounces of butter warmed. Put a crust into a shallow dish, nick the edges, and put the above into it. When served, turn the pudding out of the dish.

BAKED APPLE PUDDING.—Pare and quarter four large apples; boil them tender, with the rind of a lemon, in so little water that, when done, none may remain; beat them quite fine in a mortar; add the crumb of a small roll, four ounces of butter melted, the yolks of five and whites of three eggs, juice of half a lemon, and sugar to taste; beat all together, and lay it in a dish with paste to turn out.

BATTER PUDDING.—Rub three spoonfuls of fine flour extremely smooth by degrees into a pint of milk: simmer till it thickens, stir in two ounces of butter; set it to cool; then add the yolks of three eggs: flour a cloth that has been wet, or butter a basin, and put the batter into it; tie it tight, and plunge it into boiling water, the bottom upwards. Boil it an hour and a half, and serve with plain butter. If approved, a little ginger, nutmeg, and lemon peel may be added. Serve with sweet sauce.

BATTER PUDDING WITH MEAT.—Make a batter with flour, milk and eggs; pour a little into the bottom of a pudding-dish; then put seasoned meat of any kind into it, and a little shred onion; pour the remainder of the batter over, and bake in a slow oven. Some like a loin of mutton baked in batter, being first cleared of most of the fat.

[1867] THE RECEIPT BOOK.

GRANT & HENDERSON,

ROBERTS' NEW BLOCK, NO. 20, RIDEAU ST.,

——AND THE——

Bishop's New Building, near the Cathedral, Sussex St.

IMPORTERS OF

MILLINERY and MANTLES,
DAMASKS, FLOOR OIL-CLOTHS, BLANKETS, HOSIERY
DRY GOODS,
CARPETS,
HOUSE-FURNISHINGS, CANADIAN TWEEDS, and YARNS, &c., &c., &c.

PLAIN RICE PUDDING.—Wash and pick some rice; throw among it some pimento finely pounded, but not much; tie the rice in a cloth, and leave plenty of room for it to swell. Boil it in a quantity of water for an hour or two. When done, eat it with butter and sugar, or milk. Put lemon-peel if you please. It is very good without spice, and eaten with salt and butter.

BAKED RICE PUDDING.—Put into a very deep pan half a pound of rice washed and picked; two ounces of butter, four ounces of sugar, a few allspice pounded, and two quarts of milk. Less butter will do, or some suet. Bake in a slow oven.

SUET PUDDING.—Shred a pound of suet; mix with a pound and a quarter of flour, two eggs beaten separately, a little salt, and as little milk as will make it. Boil four hours. It eats well next day, cut in slices and broiled. The outward fat of loins or necks of mutton finely shred, makes a more delicate pudding than suet.

CUSTARD PUDDING.—Mix by degrees a pint of good milk with a large spoonful of flour, the yolks of five eggs, some orange-flower water, and a little pounded cinnamon. Butter a basin that will exactly hold it, pour the batter in, and tie a floured cloth over. Put in boiling water over the fire, and turn it about a few minutes to prevent the egg going to one side. Half an hour will boil it. Put current-jelly on it, and serve with sweet sauce.

YORKSHIRE PUDDING.—Mix five spoonfuls of flour, with a quart of milk, and three eggs well beaten. Butter the pan. When brown by baking under the meat, turn the other side upwards, and brown that. It should be made in a square pan, and cut into pieces to come to table. Set it over a chafing-dish at first, and stir it some minutes.

GRANT & HENDERSON

Have constantly on hand a Large and well assorted

Stock of

Dry Goods,

 Millinery,

  Mantles,

   Carpets,

    Floor Oil Cloths,

     Table Oil Cloths,

House Furnishing,

  Damasks,

   Cloths,

    Tweeds, &c., &c.

ESTABLISHMENTS:

Robert's New Block, No. 20, Rideau street, and the Bishop's Building, near the Cathedral, Sussex street.

COMMON PLUM PUDDING.—The same proportions of flour and suet, and half the quantity of fruit, with spice, lemon, a glass of wine or not, and one egg and milk, will make an excellent pudding, if long boiled.

COMMON PANCAKES.—Make a light batter of eggs, flour and milk. Fry in a small pan, in hot dripping or lard. Salt, or nutmeg, and ginger, may be added. Sugar and lemon should be served to eat with them. Or, when eggs are scarce, make the batter with flour, and small beer, ginger, &c.; or clean snow, with flour, and a very little milk, will serve as well as egg.

PANCAKES OF RICE.—Boil half a pound of rice to a jelly in a small quantity of water; when cold, mix it with a pint of cream, eight eggs, a bit of salt and nutmeg; stir in eight ounces of butter just warmed, and add as much flour as will make the batter thick enough. Fry in as little lard or dripping as possible.

DOMESTIC COOKERY.—VEGETABLES.

Vegetables should be carefully cleaned from insects and nicely washed. Boil them in plenty of water, and drain them the moment they are done enough. If over-boiled, they lose their beauty and crispness. Bad cooks sometimes dress them with meat, which is wrong, except carrots with boiling beef.

TO BOIL VEGETABLES GREEN.—Be sure the water boils when you put them in. Make them boil very fast. Don't cover, but watch them; and if the water has not slackened, you may be sure they are done when they begin to sink. Then take them out immediately, or the color will change. Hard water, especially if chalybeate, spoils the color of such vegetables as should be green. To boil them green in hard water, put a tea-spoonful of salt of wormwood into the water when it boils, before the vegetables are put in.

1867] THE RECEIPT BOOK. 11

OF ALL WORK BOUGHT AT THE RED BOOT

THE SEWING AND PEGGING

WILLIAM A. LAMB

Always keeps on hand a large and well-assorted stock of the Latest and Best Styles of

Boots and Shoes

OF ALL KINDS.

His Stock of Coarse Boots is large, and as Cheap as the Cheapest.

CHEAP.

His stock of fine goods for Gents, Ladies, and Children embraces all the Leading Styles.

REPAIRED FREE OF CHARGE.

THE RED BOOT.

Particular Attention is directed to the ORDERED DEPARTMENT, in which the best of material is made up by First-Class Workmen, and a fit is warranted.

GOOD.

WHOLESALE BUYERS for CASH will do well to call before making their purchases.

WM. A. LAMB,
28, Sussex St., Ottawa.

To KEEP GREEN PEAS.—Shell, and put them into a kettle of water when it boils; give them two or three walms only, and pour them into a colander. When the water drains off, turn them out on a dresser covered with cloth, and pour them on another cloth to dry perfectly. Then bottle them in wide-mouthed bottles; leaving only room to pour clarified mutton-suet upon them an inch thick, and for the cork. Rosin it down; and keep it in a cellar or in the earth, as will be directed for gooseberries under the head of keeping for Winter. When they are to be used, boil them till tender, with a bit of butter, a spoonful of sugar, and a bit of mint.

To Stew old Peas.—Steep them in water all night, if not fine boilers; otherwise only half an hour: put them into water enough just to cover them, with a good bit of butter, or a piece of beef or pork. Stew them very gently till the peas are soft, and the meat is tender; if it is not salt meat, add salt and a little pepper. Serve them round the meat.

To Stew Cucumbers.—Slice them thick; or halve and divide them into two lengths: stew some salt and pepper, and sliced onions; add a little broth, or a bit of butter. Simmer very slowly; and before serving, if no butter was in before, put some, and a little flour; or if there was butter in, only a little flour, unless it wants richness.

To Stew Onions.—Peel six large onions; fry gently of a fine brown, but do not blacken them; then put them into a small stew-pan, with a little weak gravy, pepper, and salt; cover and stew two hours gently. They should be lightly floured at first.

Roast Onions should be done with all the skins on. They eat well alone, with only salt and cold butter; or with roast potatoes; or with beet-roots.

To boil Cauliflowers.—Choose those that are close and white. Cut off the green leaves, and look carefully that there are no caterpillars about the stalk. Soak an hour in cold water; then boil them in milk and water; and take care to skim the sauce-pan, that not the least foulness may fall on the flower. It must be served very white, and rather crimp.

Spinach requires great care in washing and picking it. When that is done, throw it into a sauce-pan that will just hold it, sprinkle it with a little salt, and cover close. The pan must be set on the fire, and well shaken. When done, beat the spinach well with a small bit of butter; it must come to table pretty dry; and looks well if pressed into a tin mould in the form of a large leaf, which is sold at the tin shops. A spoonful of cream is an improvement.

To dress Beans.—Boil tender, with a bunch of parsley, which must be chopped to serve with them. Bacon or pickled pork must be served to eat with, but not boiled with them.

French Beans.—String, and cut them into four or eight; the last looks best. Lay them in salt and water; and when the sauce-pan boils, put them in with some salt. As soon as they are done, serve them immediately, to preserve the green color. Or when half-done, drain the water off, and put them into two spoonfuls of broth strained; and add a little cream, butter and flour, to finish doing them.

To Stew Red Cabbage.—Shred the cabbage; wash it and put it over a slow fire, with slices of onion, pepper, and salt, and a little plain gravy. When quite tender, and a few minutes before serving, add a bit of butter rubbed with flour, and two or three spoonfuls of vinegar, and boil up.

MORTIMER'S

Infallible Remedy for

CHOLERA, DIARRHŒA,

AND

BOWEL COMPLAINTS.

———o———

The following extract, which Mr. Mortimer is kindly permitted to publish, is from the letter of a relative of Dr. Wolf of this city, now residing in the United States :—

"Find out if the express charges are too high, and if not arrange with Mortimer to let you have a box of the bottles of CHOLERA MIXTURE. I could make a good little fortune with them. The bottle I brought with me here brought two ladies round from decided cholera: one on board the boat and the other in Berlin, United States. Both commenced with Diarrhœa, then dysentery, and then vomiting. The one at Berlin was very bad. I gave her three doses of the Cholera Mixture, the third of which stopped the vomiting. The next day she was all right or nearly so. She was very grateful. I have now only a little left."

☞ This excellent mixture, which should be in every family, is only

25 CENTS A BOTTLE.

41, SUSSEX STREET.

Mushrooms.—The cook should be perfectly acquainted with the different sort of things called by this name by ignorant people, as the death of many persons has been occasioned by carelessly using the poisonous kinds. The eatable mushrooms first appear very small, and of a round form, on a little stalk. They grow very fast, and the upper part and stalk are white. As the size increases, the under part gradually opens, and shews a fringy fur of a very fine salmon-color, which continues more or less till the mushroom has gained some size, and then turns to a dark brown. These marks should be attended to, and likewise whether the skin can be easily parted from the edges and middle. Those that have a white or yellow fur should be carefully avoided, though many of them have the same smell (but not so strong) as the right sort.

Beet-roots.—Boil the beet tender with the skin on ; slice it into a stew-pan with a little broth, and a spoonful of vinegar : simmer till the gravy is tinged with the color ; then put it into a small dish, and make a round of the bottom-onions, first boiled till tender ; take off the skin just before serving, and mind they are quite hot and clear.

To preserve several Vegetables to eat in the Winter.—For French Beans, pick them young, and throw into a little wooden keg a layer of them three inches deep ; then sprinkle them with salt, put another layer of beans, and do the same as high as you think proper, alternately with salt, but not too much of this. Lay over them a plate, or cover of wood, that will go into the keg, and put a heavy stone on it. A pickle will rise from the beans and salt. If they are too salt, the soaking and boiling will not be sufficient to make them pleasant to the taste. When they are to be eaten, cut, soak, and boil them as if fresh.

NONE OTHER GENUINE!

TRADE MARK  REGISTERED.

Canadian Cough Emulsion.

This valuable Medicine has the extraordinary property of immediately relieving Coughs, Colds, Hoarseness, Difficulty of Breathing, Tightness in the Chest, &c., &c. It operates by dissolving the congealed phlegm, causing free expectoration, and an agreeable moistness of the skin.

Those who are troubled with that unpleasant tickling in the throat, which deprives them of rest at night by the incessant cough which it provokes, will, by using this medicine, find immediate relief; and one bottle will, in most cases, effect a cure. It may be taken with perfect safety by children of three or four years of age. Prepared only by

GEORGE MORTIMER,
CHEMIST AND DRUGGIST,
41, SUSSEX STREET, OTTAWA CITY.

Sold in bottles at 1s. 3d. and 2s. 6d. each.

MORTIMER's COMPOUND ANTIBILIOUS
AND FAMILY APERIENT PILLS,

A Grand Specific for derangement of the Digestive Organs, and for obstructions and torpid action of the Liver and Bowels.

MORTIMER'S VEGETABLE WORM DESTROYER.

The only sure Remedy that exists. Combining Delicious Taste and Amazing Power.

41, SUSSEX STREET.

Carrots, Parsnips and Beet-roots, should be kept in layers of dry sand for winter-use; and neither they nor potatoes should be cleared from the earth. Potatoes should be carefully kept from frost.

Store-onions keep best hung up in a dry cold room.

Parsley should be cut close to the stalks; and dried in a warm room, or on tins in a very cool oven: it preserves its flavor and color, and is very useful in winter.

Small close Cabbages, laid on a stone floor before the frost sets in, will blanch and be very fine, after many weeks keeping.

Pickles.—Keep them closely covered; and have a wooden spoon, with hold tied to each jar; all metal being improper. They should be well kept from the air; the large jars be seldom opened; and small ones, for the different pickles in use, should be kept for common supply, into which what is not eaten may be returned, and the top closely covered.

Acids dissolve the lead that is in the tinning of saucepans. When necessary to boil vinegar, do it in a stone jar, on the hot hearth. Pickles should never be put into glazed jars, as salt and vinegar penetrate the glaze, which is poisonous.

An excellent way to pickle Mushrooms, to preserve the Flavor.—Buttons must be rubbed with a bit of flannel and salt; and from the larger, take out the red inside, for when they are black they will not do, being too old. Throw a little salt over, and put them into a stew pan with some mace and pepper; as the liquor comes out, shake them well, and keep them over a gentle fire till all of it be dried into them again; then put as much vinegar into the pan as will cover them, give it one warm, and turn all into a glass or stone jar. They will keep two years, and are delicious.

1867]   THE RECEIPT BOOK.   19

VERDICT IN FAVOR of THE TEA POT!

ESTABLISHMENTS: Union Block, Sussex St., Rideau Street and Wellington Street.

Some dealers in Tea, Sugar, Coffee and Spices,
From various causes were vieing in prices,
Till rivalry into fierce quarrel was veering,
Which timely was checked by some stranger appearing,
"Fie! Fie!" he exclaimed, let this quarrelling cease,
Your passions restrain and disturb not the peace;
Low PRICES 'tis folly to quarrel about,
'Tis QUALITY, only, that's worth finding out—
Let's fairly and calmly put that to the test,
And we shall find out the cheapest and best;
And, when 'tis decided, proclaimed let it be,
Who sells the best Coffee and who the best Tea."
The plan was approved of, and judges elected,
Whose honest opinions had ne'er been suspected;
When this Tea and that Tea they tasted in turn,
And then tried the Coffee from out a new urn—
And in a few seconds returned to decide:
" Unbiassed and void of all prejudice we,
Unite in asserting that ROBINSON'S TEA
We've put in each possible way to the test,
And find it to be really the CHEAPEST and BEST;
And as for their COFFEES, we also declare
Such Coffee is not to be met with elsewhere."
Thus calmly was ended a noisy affray,
And Robinson's Teas are the theme of the day.

   ROBINSON & Co., The Tea Pot, Ottawa.

DIRECTIONS FOR MAKING TEA.—First—See that the water boils before you attempt to brew the Tea. Second—Never use hard water—it will spoil the best tea. If you cannot obtain soft water, put in a small piece of Baking Soda, about the size of a pea, into the Tea Pot, and you will find your Tea better and stronger. Third—Attend to these directions, get your Tea from THE TEA POT, in Ottawa, and you will always have A CUP OF GOOD TEA.

Pickled Onions.—In the month of September, choose the small white round onions, take off the brown skin, have ready a very nice tin stew pan of boiling water, throw in as many onions as will cover the top; as soon as they look clear on the outside, take them up as quick as possible with a slice, and lay them on a clean cloth; cover them close with another, and scald some more, and so on. Let them lie to be cold, then put them in a jar, or glass wide-mouth bottles, and pour over them the best white wine vinegar, just hot, but not boiling. When cold, cover them. Should the other skin shrivel, peel it off. They must look quite clear.

To pickle Cucumbers and Onions sliced.—Cut them in slices, and sprinkle salt over them: next day drain them for five or six hours; then put them into a stone jar, pour boiling vinegar over them, and keep them in a warm place. The slices should be thick. Repeat the boiling vinegar, and stop them up again instantly; and so on till green; the last time put pepper and ginger. Keep it in small stone jars.

To pickle Red Cabbage.—Slice it into a colander, and sprinkle each layer with salt; let it drain two days, then put it into a jar, and pour boiling vinegar enough to cover, and put a few slices of red beet-root. Observe to choose the purple red cabbage. Those who like the flavor of spice will boil it with the vinegar. Cauliflower cut in branches, and thrown in after being salted, will look of a beautiful red.

Buttered Rice.—Wash and pick some rice, drain, and put it with some new milk, enough just to swell it, over the fire; when tender, pour off the milk, and add a bit of butter, a little sugar, and pounded cinnamon. Shake it, that it do not burn, and serve.

GOOD TEA!
And Where to get It!

---o---

O, come awa' with me, guidwife,
  Just come awa' with me;
I'll lead you on to the best shop
  For selling Splendid Tea.
      In Sussex Street you'll get the place,
        So don't wait, but look alive;
      You'll find the Tea Pot above the door,
        The number's forty-five.

The toothache put my wife near daft,
  The pain was unco sair;
She took a cup of "Tea Pot's" Tea,
  It cured her, I declare.
      Their Tea is meat and medicine,
        Their customers all say;
      It cheers the heart when it is sad,
        It makes the spirits gay.

Then gong ye a' to Tea Pot's shop,
  Ye'll ne'er deceived be,
Their goods are all so very cheap,
  As well their charming Tea.

        JAS. G. ROBINSON, & Co.,
                The Tea Pot, Ottawa.

ESTABLISHMENTS.—Sussex Street, Rideau Street, Wellington Street.

To pickle Butternuts.—When they will bear a pin to go into them, put a brine of salt and water boiled, and strong enough to bear an egg on them, being quite cold first. It must be well skimmed while boiling. Let them soak six days; then change the brine, let them stand six more; then drain them, and pour over them in the jar a pickle of the best white wine vinegar, with a good quantity of pepper, pimento, ginger, mace, cloves, mustard-seed, and horse-radish; all boiled together, but cold. To every hundred of butternuts put six spoonfuls of mustard seed, and two or three heads of garlic or shalot, but the latter is least strong.

Mushroom Ketchup.—Take the largest broad mushrooms, break them into an earthen pan, strew salt over; and stir them now and then for three days. Then let them stand for twelve, till there is a thick scum over; strain, and boil the liquor with Jamaica and black peppers, mace, ginger, a clove or two, and some mustard seed. When cold, bottle it, and tie a bladder over the cork; in three months boil it again with some fresh spice, and it will then keep a twelvemonth.

Snow-balls.—Swell rice in milk, strain it off, and having pared and cored apples, put the rice round them, tying each up in a cloth. Put a bit of lemon-peel, a clove or cinnamon in each, and boil them well.

Gooseberry Fool—Put the fruit into a stone jar, and some sugar; set the jar on a stove, or in a saucepan of water over the fire; if the former, a large spoonful of water should be added to the fruit. When it is done enough to pulp, press it through a colander; have ready a sufficient quantity of new milk, a tea-cup of raw cream, boiled together; or an egg instead of the latter, and left to be cold; then sweeten it pretty well with fine sugar, and mix the pulp by degrees with it.

1867] THE RECEIPT BOOK. 23

E. SPENCER,
PHOTOGRAPHER,
24, SPARKS STREET, CENTRAL OTTAWA.

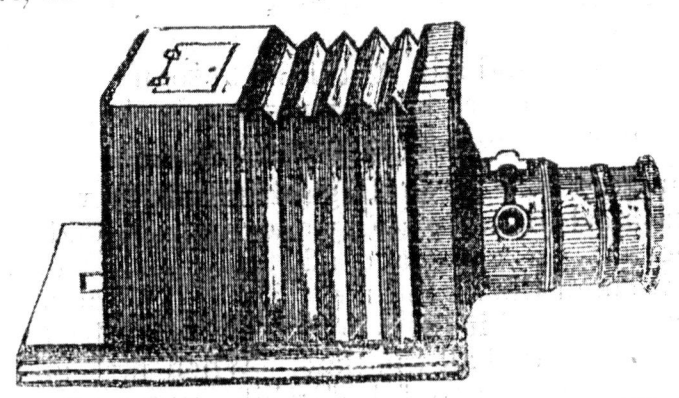

SIGN OF THE CAMERA.
—o—
PHOTOGRAPHS OF ALL SIZES.
FROM THE
MINIATURE GEM TO SIZE OF LIFE.

Particular attention paid to Cartes de Visites or Album Pictures, which are sent by mail, prepaid, to any part of Canada, if desired.

First-Class Workmen Constantly Employed.

He would call particular attention to his Stereoscopic and other Views of PARLIAMENT BUILDINGS and OTTAWA SCENERY, of which he has a large variety constantly on hand, for sale.

N. B.—The Trade supplied with Stereoscopic and other views at very reasonable rates.

☞ CALL AND SEE.

Apple Fool—Stew apples as directed for gooseberries, and then peel and pulp them. Prepare the milk, &c., and mix as before.

Orange Fool—Mix the juice of three Seville oranges. three eggs well beaten, a pint of cream, a little nutmeg and cinnamon, and sweeten to your taste. Set the whole over a slow fire, and stir it till it becomes as thick as good melted butter, but it must not be boiled; then pour it into a dish for eating cold.

Flummery—Put three large handfuls of very small white oatmeal to steep a day and night in cold water; then pour it off clear, and add as much more water and let it stand the same time. Strain it through a fine hair seive, and boil it till it be as thick as hasty pudding; stirring it well all the time. When first strained, put to it one large spoonful of white sugar, and two of orange-flower water. Pour it into shallow dishes, and serve to eat with wine, cider, milk, or cream and sugar. It is very good.

Black Caps.—Take off a slice from the stock end of some apples, and core without paring them. Make ready as much sugar as may be sufficient to sweeten them, and mix with some grated lemon, and a few cloves in fine powder. Stuff the holes as close as possible with this, and turn the flat end down on a stewpan; set them on a very slow fire, with half of raisin wine, and the same of water: cover them close, and now and then baste them with the liquor; when done enough, black the tops with a salamander.

Welch Rabbit.—Toast a slice of bread on both sides, and butter it; toast a slice of cheese on one side, and lay that next the bread, and toast the other side with a salamander; rub mustard over and serve very hot, and covered.

1867]   THE RECEIPT BOOK.

THE NEW SIZE!

—O R—

CABINET PHOTOGRAPH!

The subscriber would take this method of intimating that he has lately introduced the above size and style of Photograph into his Gallery; also a fine assortment of Albums to suit them. And he has also, at considerable expense, added to his Gallery a new POSING APPARATUS, by the use of which a variety of graceful and easy positions may be obtained, thereby avoiding the stiffness and sameness which unavoidably occur in using the old style of head-rest.

A trial will convince any one of its superiority, both as to comfort in sitting, and grace and elegance of position.

The new size Photograph is a much more pleasing picture than the common card, being nearly four times as large, and only twice the cost. It makes a nice picture for framing, and is in fact the nicest size and style that has yet been introduced.

Call and see for yourself, at the old stand,

SIGN OF THE CAMERA.

24 SPARKS STREET.

E. SPENCER.

Stewed Pears.—Pare and halve, or quarter, large pears, according to their size ; throw them into water, as the skin is taken off before they are divided, to prevent their turning black. Pack them round a block-tin stew pan, and sprinkle as much sugar over them as will make them sweet, and add lemon peel, a clove or two, and some allspice cracked; just cover them with water, and put some of the red liquor, as directed in another article. Cover them close, and stew three or four hours ; when tender, take them out and pour the liquor over them.

Baked Pears—These need not be of a fine sort ; but some taste better than others, and often those that are least fit to eat raw. Wipe, but DON'T pare, and lay them on tin plates, and bake them in a slow oven. When done enough to bear it, flatten them with a silver spoon. When done through, put them on a dish. They should be baked three or four times, and very gently.

To Prepare Fruit for Children, a far more wholesome way than in Pies and Puddings.—Put apples sliced, or plums, currants, gooseberries, &c., into a stone jar, and sprinkle as much sugar as necessary among them; set the jar on a hot hearth, or in a saucepan of water, and let it remain till the fruit is perfectly done. Slices of bread, or rice, may be either stewed with the fruit, or added when eaten ; the rice being plain boiled.

To dry Cherries without Sugar.—Stone, and set them over the fire in the preserving-pan ; let them simmer in their own liquor, and shake them in the pan. Put them by in china common dishes; next day give them another scald, and put them, when cold, on sieves to dry, in an oven of attemperated heat as above. Twice heating, an hour each time, will do them. Put them in a box, with a paper between each layer.

[1867] THE RECEIPT BOOK.

SHEFFIELD HOUSE,

24, SPARKS STREET, OTTAWA

E. K. McGillivray & Co.,

WATCHMAKERS & JEWELLERS,

Direct Importers of

Watches, Clocks, Jewellery, Electro-Plated Ware, Fancy Goods, Papier Machie and Cabinetware, Dressing Cases, Rodgers Table and Pocket Cutlery, Cricketing Material, Fishing Tackle, Croquet Archery, &c., &c.

☞ Particular attention paid to the Manufacturing and Repairing Department.

Syllabub—Put a pint and a half of port or white wine into a bowl, nutmeg grated, and a good deal of sugar, then milk into it near two quarts of milk, frothed up. If the wine be not rather sharp, it will require more for this quantity of milk. In Devonshire, clouted cream is put on the top, and pounded cinnamon and sugar.

Macaroni—Boil it in milk, or weak veal broth, pretty well flavored with salt. When tender, put it into a dish without the liquor, and among it put some bits of butter and grated cheese, and over the top grate more, and a little more butter. Set the dish into a Dutch oven a quarter of an hour, but do not let the top become hard.

Omlet.—Make a batter of eggs and milk, and a very little flour; put to it chopped parsley, green onions, or chives (the latter is best), or a very small quantity of shalot, a little pepper, salt, and a scrape or two of nutmeg. Make some butter boil in a small frying-pan, and pour the above liquor into it; when one side is of a fine yellow brown, turn it and do the other. Double it when served. Some scraped lean ham, or grated tongue, put in at first, is a very pleasant addition. Four eggs will make a pretty sized omlet; but many cooks will use eight or ten. A small proportion of flour should be used.

To Candy any sort of Fruit.—When finished in the syrup, put a layer into a new sieve, and dip it suddenly into hot water, to take off the syrup that hangs about it; put it on a napkin before the fire to drain, and then do some more in the sieve. Have ready sifted double-refined sugar, which sift over the fruit on all sides till quite white. Set it on the shallow end of sieves in a slightly-warm oven, and turn it two or three times. It must not be cold till dry. Watch it carefully, and it will be beautiful.

BROWNE & HARDY,

GENERAL GROCERS,

WINE AND SPIRIT MERCHANTS,

DEALERS IN

PORK, FLOUR, FISH,

&c., &c.

NO. 16, RIDEAU STREET.

D. T. BROWNE.   R. H. HARDY.

To preserve Suet a Twelvemonth.—As soon as it comes in, choose the firmest part, and pick free from skin and veins. In a very nice sauce-pan, set it at some distance from the fire, that it may melt without frying, or it will taste. When melted, pour it into a pan of cold water. When in a hard cake, wipe it very dry, fold it in fine paper, and then in a linen bag, and keep in a dry but not hot place. When used, scrape it fine, and it will make a fine crust, either with or withour butter.

Peaches in Brandy.—Wipe, weigh and pick the fruit, and have ready a quarter of the weight of fine sugar in fine powder. Put the fruit into an ice-pot that shuts very close; throw the sugar over it, and then cover the fruit with brandy. Between the top and cover of the pot, put a piece of double cap-paper. Set the pot into a sauce-pan of water till the brandy be as hot as you can possibly bear to put your finger in, but it must not boil. Put the fruit into a jar, and pour the brandy on it. When cold, put a bladder over, and tie it down tight.

Currant Jelly, Red or Black.—Strip the fruit, and in a stone jar stew them in a sauce-pan of water, or by boiling it on the hot earth; strain off the liquor, and to every pint weigh a pound of loaf-sugar; put the latter in large lumps into it, in a stone or china vessel, till nearly dissolved; then put it in a preserving-pan; simmer and skim as necessary. When it will jelly on a plate, put it in small jars or glasses.

Apple Marmalade.—Scald apples till they will pulp from the core; then take an equal weight of sugar in large lumps, just dip them in water, and boiling it till it can be well skimmed, and is a thick syrup, put to it the pulp, and simmer it on a quick fire a quarter of an hour. Grate a little lemon-peel before boiled, but if too much it will be bitter.

SHEFFIELD HOUSE,

24, SPARKS STREET, OTTAWA.

E. K. McGILLIVRAY & CO.,

MANUFACTURERS AND IMPORTERS OF

MASONIC JEWELS!

Watches, Clocks, Jewellery, Electro-Plated Ware, Fancy Goods, Rodgers Table and Pocket Cutlery, English, French, and German Fancy Goods, Small Wares, &c., &c.

WATCHES, CLOCKS, AND JEWELLERY

Carefully Repaired and Warranted.

Orange Marmalade.—Rasp the oranges, cut out the pulp, then boil the rinds very tender, and beat fine in a marble mortar. Boil three pounds of loaf-sugar in a pint of water, skim it, and add a pound of the rind; boil fast till the syrup is very thick, but stir it carefully; then put a pint of the pulp and juice, the seeds having been removed, and a pint of apple liquor; boil all gently until well jellied, which it will be in about half an hour. Put it into small pots.

Lemon marmalade do in the same way; they are very good and elegant sweetmeats.

To dry Cherries with sugar.—Stone six pounds of cherries; put them into a preserving-pan, with two pounds of loaf-sugar pounded and strewed among them; simmer till they begin to shrivel; then strain them from the juice; lay them on a hot hearth, or in an oven, when either is cool enough to dry without baking them. The same syrup will do another six pounds of fruit.

To preserve Strawberries whole.—Take equal weights of the fruit and double refined sugar; lay the former in a large dish, and sprinkle half the sugar, in fine powder over; give a gentle shake to the dish, that the sugar may touch the under side of the fruit. Next day make a thin syrup with the remainder of the sugar, and, instead of water, allow one pint of red current juice to every pound of strawberries; in this simmer them until sufficiently jellied. Choose the largest scarlets, or others, when not dead ripe. In either of the above ways, they eat well served in thin cream, in glasses.

Dried Apples.—Put them into a cool oven six or seven times, and flatten them by degrees, and gently, when soft enough to bear it. If the oven be too hot they will waste, and at first it should be very cool.

The Ottawa Citizen
STEAM PRINTING HOUSE!

Is replete with every requisite and appliance for the execution of

CHEAP, NEAT AND EXPEDITIOUS PRINTING!

Mammoth, Medium, and Small Posters,
Hand Bills, Concert Bills, Railroad Bills, Show Bills,
Stage Bills, and Steamboat Bills, Show Bills,
Cheque Books, Business Cards, Professional Cards,
Funeral Cards,
Wedding Cards, Tickets, &c.,
Law Blanks, Municipal and Corporation Blanks,
Promissory Note Books, &c.,
Printed in Black, Red, Blue, and other Colored Inks, and on White and Colored Paper.

—:o:—

BOOK-BINDING, BLANK BOOKS & PAPER RULING
IN EVERY STYLE.

—:o:—

CHEAPNESS, NEATNESS and PUNCTUALITY are the Principal Features of the Establishment.

Orders sent by Mail Carefully and promptly attended to, and Work despatched by Parcel Post without delay.

I. B. TAYLOR, Proprietor.

B

Gooseberry Jam for Tarts.—Gather your gooseberries (the clear white or green sort) when ripe; top and tail, and weigh them; a pound to three-quarters of a pound of fine sugar, and half a pint of water; boil and skim the sugar and water; then put the fruit, and boil gently till clear; then break and put into small pots.

Raspberry Jam.—Weigh equal quantities of fruit and sugar; put the former into a preserving-pan, boil and break it, stir constantly, and let it boil very quickly. When most of the juice is wasted, add the sugar, and simmer half an hour.

To Preserve Fruits for Winter Use.—Sweetmeats should be kept carefully from the hair, and in a very dry place. Unless they have a very small proportion of sugar, a warm one does not hurt; but when not properly boiled, that is, long enough, but not quick, heat makes them ferment; and damp causes them to grow mouldy. They should be looked at two or three times in the first two months, that they may be gently boiled again, if not likely to keep.

To Keep Gooseberries.—Before they become too large, let them be gathered, and take care not to cut them in taking off the stalks and buds. Fill wide-mouthed bottles; put the corks loosely in, and set the bottles up to the neck in water in a boiler. When the fruit looks scalded, take them out; and when perfectly cold, cork close, and rosin the top. Dig a trench in a part of the garden least used, sufficiently deep for all the bottles to stand, and let the earth be thrown over, to cover them a foot and a half. When a frost comes on, a little fresh litter from the stable will prevent the ground from hardening so that the fruit cannot be dug up. Or, scald as above; when cold, fill the bottles with cold water, cork them, and keep them in a damp or dry place; they will not be spoiled.

[1867]

CUNNINGHAM & LINDSAY,

14 Rideau Street, Ottawa,

IMPORTERS OF FANCY & STAPLE

DRY GOODS,

Have always on hand a large assortment of

Cloths, Flannels, Blankets, Dress Goods,

SILKS, SHAWLS, MANTLES, MILLINERY

FLOWERS AND FEATHERS,

Ribbons, Hosiery and Gloves, Smallwares, Haberdashery.

As the above goods are purchased in the best English and Continental Markets by one of the firm, customers can rely on getting always the latest styles and best value.

To Keep Currants.—The bottles being perfectly clean and dry, let the currants be cut from the large stalks with the smallest bit of stalk to each, that the fruit not being wounded no moisture may be among them. It is necessary to gather them when the weather is quite dry; and if the servant can be depended upon, it is best to cut them under the trees, and let them drop gently into the bottles. Stop up the bottles with cork and rosin, and put them into the trench in the garden with the neck downwards; sticks should be placed opposite to where each sort of fruit begins.

To Keep Plums for Winter Pies.—Put them in small stone jars, or wide-mouthed bottles; set them up to their necks in a boiler of cold water, and lighting a fire under, scald them. Next day, when perfectly cold, fill up with spring water; cover them. Boil one third as much sugar as fruit with it, over a slow fire, till the juice adheres to the fruit, and forms a jam. Keep it in small jars in a dry place. If too sweet, mix with it some of the fruit that is done without sugar.

Iceing for Cakes.—For a large one, beat and sift eight ounces of fine sugar, put into a mortar, with four spoonfuls of rose-water, and the whites of two eggs beaten and strained, whisk it well, and when the cake is almost cold, dip a feather in the iceing, and cover the cake well; set it in the oven to harden, but don't let it stay to discolor. Put the cake into a dry place.

Very good Common Plum Cakes.—Mix five ounces of butter in three pounds of dry flour, and five ounces of fine sugar; add six ounces of currants, washed and dried, and some pimento finely powdered. Put three spoonfuls of yeast into a Winchester pint of new milk warmed, and mix into a light dough with the above. Make it into twelve cakes, and bake on a floured tin half an hour.

1867] THE RECEIPT BOOK. 37

CAMPBELL & SLEEMAN,

AT

THE OLD SIGN OF CAMPBELL & CO.,

Sussex Street, Lower Town.

THERE YOU WILL FIND THE CHEAPEST

GROCERIES AND LIQUORS

IN THE CITY.

☞ Call and satisfy yourselves.
Don't forget the Sign,

CAMPBELL & Co.

Observations on Making and Baking Cakes.—Currants should be very nicely washed, dried in a cloth, and then set before the fire. If damp they will make cakes or puddings heavy. Before they are added, a dust of dry flour should be thrown among them, and a shake given to them, which causes the thing that they are put to, to be lighter. Eggs should be very long beaten, whites and yolks apart, and always strained. Sugar should be rubbed to a powder on a clean board, and sifted through a very fine hair or lawn-sieve. Lemon-peel should be pared very thin, and with a little sugar beaten in a marble mortar to a paste, and then mixed with a little wine or cream, so as to divide easily among the other ingredients. After all the articles are put into the pan, they should be thoroughly and long beaten, as the lightness of the cake depends much on their being well incorporated. The heat of the oven is of great importance for cakes, especially those that are large. If not pretty quick, the batter will not rise. Should you fear its catching by being too quick, put some paper over the cake to prevent its being burnt. If not long enough lighted to have a body of heat, or it is become slack, the cake will be heavy. To know when it is soaked, take a broad-bladed knife that is very bright, and plunge it into the very centre, draw it instantly out, and if the least stickiness adheres, put the cake immediately in, and shut up the oven. If the heat was sufficient to raise, but not to soak, I have with great success had fresh fuel quickly put in, and kept the cakes hot till the oven was fit to finish the soaking, and they turned out extremely well. But those who are employed, ought to be particularly careful that no mistake occur from negligence when large cakes are to be baked.

1867]   THE RECEIPT BOOK.   3

NO. 24.   **NO. 24.**

SIGN OF   **THE ANVIL,**

Rideau   Street.

THOMAS BIRKETT,

(SUCCESSOR TO JAS. STARKE,)

General Dealer in Shelf & Heavy Hardware,

STOVES, IRON, COALS,

ROPES, CHAINS, SAWS,

AXES, &c., &c., &c.

Also, GLASS, PAINT, OILS,

PUTTY, &c., &c.

Raspberry Vinegar.—Put a pound of fine fruit into a china bowl, and pour upon it a quart of the best white wine vinegar; next day strain the liquor on a pound of fresh raspberries; and the following day do the same, but do not squeeze the fruit, only drain the liquor as dry as you can from it. The last time pass it through a canvass previously wet with vinegar to prevent waste. Put it into a stone jar, with a pound of sugar to every pint of juice, broken into large lumps; stir it when melted, then put the jar into a sauce-pan of water, or on a hot hearth, let it simmer, and skim it. When cold bottle it.

Little Plum Cakes, to Keep Long.—Dry one pound of flour, and mix with six ounces of finely pounded sugar, beat six ounces of butter to a cream, and add to three eggs, well beaten, half a pound of currants washed, and nicely dried, and the flour and sugar; beat all for some time, then dredge flour on tin plates, and drop the batter on them the size of a walnut. If properly mixed, will be a stiff paste. Bake in a brisk oven.

A Cheap Seed Cake.—Mix a quarter of a peck of flour with half a pound of sugar, a quarter of an ounce of all spice, and a little ginger; melt three quarters of a pound of butter, with half a pint of milk; when just warm put to it a quarter of a pint of yeast, and work up to a good dough. Let it stand before the fire a few minutes before it goes to the oven; add seeds or currents, and bake an hour and a half.

Common Bread Cake.—Take the quantity of a quarter loaf from the dough, when making white bread, and knead well into it two ounces of butter, two of Lisbon sugar, and eight of currents. Warm the butter in a tea-cupful of good milk.

1867]   THE RECEIPT BOOK.

ELLIOTT & HAMILTON,

DEALERS IN

FANCY AND STAPLE DRY GOODS!

DRESS GOODS,	SILKS,	FLANNELS,
SHAWLS,	RIBBONS,	BLANKETS,
HOSIERY,	LACES,	COTTONS,
GLOVES,	FLOWERS,	LINENS,
WINCEYS,	PLUMES,	CLOTHS,
HOOP SKIRTS,	CLOUDS,	TWEEDS,

CANADIAN WOOLLEN YARNS,

Canadian Knitted Underclothing, and

BEST COTTON WARPS.

ELLIOTT & HAMILTON,

No. 23 Rideau Street.

A Good Pound Cake.—Beat a pound of butter to a cream, and mix with it the whites and yolks of eight eggs beaten apart. Have ready warm by the fire, a pound of flour, and the same of sifted sugar, mix them and a few cloves, a little nutmeg and cinnamon in fine powder together; then by degrees work the dry ingredients into the butter and eggs. When well beaten, add a glass of wine and some caraways. It must be beaten a full hour. Butter a pan, and bake it a full hour in a quick oven. The above proportions, leaving out four ounces of the butter, and the same of sugar, make a less luscious cake, and to most tastes a more pleasant one.

Another way.—Beat eight ounces of butter, and mix with two well-beaten eggs, strained; mix eight ounces of dried flour, and the same of lump-sugar, and the grated rind of a lemon, then add the whole together, and beat full half an hour with a silver spoon. Butter small pattypans, half fill, and bake twenty minutes in a quick oven.

Sponge Cake.—Weigh ten eggs, and their weight in very fine sugar, and that of six in flour; beat the yolks with the flour, and the whites alone to a very stiff froth; then by degrees mix the whites and the flour with the other ingredients, and beat them well half an hour. Bake in a quick oven an hour. Another way, without batter:—Dry one pound of flour and one and a quarter of sugar; beat seven eggs, yolks and whites apart; grate a lemon, and, with a spoonful of brandy, beat the whole together with your hand for an hour. Bake in a buttered pan, in a quick oven. Sweetmeats may be added, if approved.

A Biscuit Cake.—One pound of flour, five eggs well beaten and strained, eight ounces of sugar, a little rose or orange-flower water; beat the whole thoroughly, and bake one hour.

1867]   THE RECEIPT BOOK.

THOS. & WM. HUNTON,

IMPORTERS AND DEALERS IN

Fancy & Staple Dry Goods,

CARPETS AND HOUSE FURNISHINGS, &c.,

MANUFACTURERS OF CLOTHING,

47 AND 49 SPARKS STREET,

OTTAWA,

Respectfully invite an inspection of their

LARGE & VARIED STOCK

In which will always be found

EVERY NOVELTY OF THE SEASON,

At as low, or lower, prices than any other house in Canada.

Tea Cakes.—Rub fine four ounces of butter into eight ounces of flour; mix eight ounces of currants, and six of fine sugar, two yolks and one white of eggs, and a spoonful of brandy. Roll the paste the thickness of an Oliver biscuit, and cut with a wine glass. You may beat the other white, and wash over them; and either dust sugar, or not, as you like.

A Good Plain Bun.—Rub four ounces of butter into two pounds of flour, four ounces of sugar, a nutmeg, or not, as you like, a few Jamaica peppers, a desert spoonful of caraways; put a spoonful or two of cream into a cup of yeast, and as much good milk as will make the above into a light paste. Set it to rise by the fire till the oven be ready. They will quickly bake on tins.

Gingerbread.—Mix with two pounds of flour half a pound of treacle, three quarters of an ounce of caraways, one ounce of ginger finely sifted, and eight ounces of butter. Roll the paste into what form you please, and bake on tins, after having worked it very much, and kept it to rise.

Muffins.—Mix two pounds of flour with two eggs, two ounces of butter melted in a pint of milk, and four or five spoonfuls of yeast: beat it thoroughly, and set it to rise two or three hours. Bake on a hot hearth in flat cakes. When done on one side turn them.

Hard Biscuits.—Warm two ounces of butter in as much skimmed milk as will make a pound of flour into a very stiff paste, beat it with a rolling pin, and work it very smooth. Roll it thin, and cut it into round biscuits; prick them full of holes with a fork. About six minutes will bake them.

RUSSELL HOUSE,

OTTAWA.

James A Gouin, - - *Proprietor.*

Plain and very Crisp Biscuits.—Make a pound of flour the yolk of an egg, and some milk into a very stiff paste beat it well, and knead till quite smooth; roll very thin and cut into biscuits. Bake them in a slow oven till quite dry and crisp.

HOME BREWERY, WINES, &c.

To Refine Cider.—Put two ounces of isinglass shavings to soak in a quart of the liquor that you want to clear beat it with a whisk every day till dissolved. Draw off third part of the cask, and mix the above with it; likewise a quarter of an ounce of pearl-ashes, one ounce of salt of tartar calcined, and one ounce of burnt alum powdered. Stir it well, then return the liquor into the cask, and stir it with a clean stick. Stop it up, and in a few days it will be fine.

Raspberry Wine.—To every quart of well-picked raspberries put a quart of water; bruise, and let them stand two days; strain off the liquor, and to every gallon put three pounds of lump sugar; when dissolved put the liquor in a barrel, and when fine, which will be in about two months, bottle it, and to each bottle put a spoonful of brandy, or a glass of wine.

Currant Wine.—To every three pints of fruit, carefully cleared from mouldy or bad, put one quart of water; bruise the former. In twenty-four hours strain the liquor, and put to every quart a pound of sugar, of good middling quality. If for white currants, use lump sugar. It is best to put the fruit, &c., in a large pan, and when in three or four days the scum rises, take that off before the liquor be put into a barrel.

867] THE RECEIPT BOOK. 47

S. & H. BORBRIDGE,

MANUFACTURERS OF

SADDLES, HARNESS, TRUNKS,

VALISES, &C., &C.,

CORNER OF RIDEAU AND MOSGROVE STREETS,

Constantly on hand all descriptions of Satchels, Carpet Oil Cloth and Pellisier Bags, Walking Canes, Chamois Skins, Brushes, Curry Combs, Snaps, Bitts, Whips, Whip-Lashes, Nett Covers, Rowlers, Mane Combs, Clipping Scissors, Spoke Brushes, Burnishers, Elastic Horse Shoes, &c., &c.

A large assortment of

HORSE CLOTHING

constantly on hand.

The above are all offered at the lowest possible prices.

Call and Examine for Yourselves.

Black Currant Wine, very fine.—To every three quarts of juice, put the same of water unboiled; and to every three quarts of the liquor, add three pounds of very pure moist sugar. Put it into a cask, reserving a little for filling up. Put the cask in a warm dry room, and the liquor will ferment of itself. Skim off the refuse, when the fermentation shall be over, and fill up with reserved liquor. When it has ceased working, pour three quarts of brandy to forty quarts of wine. Bung it close for nine months, then bottle it, and drain the thick part through a jelly-bag, until it be clear, and bottle that. Keep it ten or twelve months.

Excellent Ginger Wine.—Put into a very nice boiler ten gallons of water, fifteen pounds of lump-sugar, with the whites of six or eight eggs well beaten and strained; mix all well while cold; when the liquor boils skim it well; put in half a pound of common white ginger bruised, boil it twenty minutes. Have ready the very thin rinds of seven lemons, and pour the liquor on them. When cool, tun it with two spoonfuls of yeast; put a quart of the liquor to two ounces of isinglass shavings, while warm, whisk it well three or four times, and pour all together into the barrel. Next day stop it up; in three weeks bottle, and in three months it will be a delicious and refreshing liquor; and though very cool, perfectly safe.

RECEIPTS FOR DYEING.

Madder Red.—Use 1 lb. Madder with 2 oz. Com. to every 2 lb. cloth or yarn. Soak the Madder over night in a brass or copper kettle; then add the com. and stir; then the cloth, and bring your dye slowly to a scalding heat; vary the time as you wish the color.

THE MEDICAL HALL!

Drugs and Chemicals.

DYE STUFFS
CAN BE HAD
CHEAP AND RELIABLE,

From me, accompanied with instructions how to use them, most of which Receipts can be seen in this Book.

CALL AT AUSTIN'S,

SIGN of 'THE GOLD MORTAR,'

Mosgrove's Block, opposite Whyte's Paper Warehouse.

Horse and Cattle Medicines of every description.

☞ Don't mistake "Sign of the Golden Mortar" over the door.

C. AUSTIN.

Black—On Wool, Silk, or Cotton.—For every lb. of cloth or yarn, it will require one oz. of the extract of Logwood and half an ounce of blue virtrol. Prepare an iron kettle with a sufficient quantity of soft water to prevent the cloth or yarn from being crowded—bring the water to a scalding heat—then put in the yarn or cloth, and when thoroughly wet take it out and let it drain; then add the blue vitriol, and when dissolved, and the water carefully skimmed, put in the material to be colored, and let it remain half an hour at a scalding heat, airing it occasionally, then take it out and rinse it in soft water. Empty the vitrol water into another vessel and dissolve the extract of logwood in a sufficient quantity of water, brought to a scalding heat and skimmed; put in the cloth, keeping the dye at the same temperature, and let it remain half an hour, airing it frequently, then take out and drain it, add the vitrol water to the dye, put it in again, and let it remain fifteen minutes, airing as before; clense it thoroughly in soft water; let it drain and dry.

Brown.—For each lb. of wool take ¼ lb. Alum and 2 oz. Cream of Tartar, and boil for half an hour. Take ½ lb. Red Powder, ¼ lb. Fustic, and 2 oz. Logwood. Soak these a night in sufficient warm water to color the wool. Take the wool out of the alum water and boil with the woods for about half an hour. If a dark brown is wanted, add a table-spoonful of copperas.

A Permanent Blue.—Boil the cloth in a brass kettle for an hour, in a solution containing five parts of alum and three of tartar for every 32 parts of cloth. It is then thrown into warm water, previously mixed with a greater or less proportion of Chemic Blue according to the shade the cloth is intended to receive. In this water it must be boiled till it has acquired the desired color.

1867] THE RECEIPT BOOK. 51

WHITESIDE & WALKER,

WHOLESALE AND RETAIL MANUFACURERS OF

SPRING BEDS,

Mattresses, Children's Carriages, Invalid Chairs, etc., etc.

We guarantee every Mattrass made by us to be
FIRST QUALITY HAIR.

Old Mattresses Made as Good as New,

AND CLEANSED FROM ALL IMPURITIES BY STEAM.

CITY EXPRESS.

Proprietors of the CITY EXPRESS and FURNITURE VANS, for the removal of Household Effects and Merchandize.

PIANOS MOVED, UNPACKED AND SET UP

By experienced hands.

PARTICULAR ATTENTION PAID TO THE PACKING OF PIANOS AND FURNITURE.

WHITESIDE & WALKER,
65 RIDEAU STREET, OTTAWA

Blue.—A rich and bright blue may be made in the following manner: Take water enough to cover the yarn, and when at the boiling point add Chemic Blue till the desired shade is obtained; boil a few minutes, note the quantity of Chemic used, and add half as much blue mordant, which will produce a most beautiful sky Napoleon or Royal Blue, according to the amount of Chemic.

Scarlet Red.—To 1 lb. cloth, 2 oz. powder Lack, 3 oz. Madder Compound; mix the two last in an earthen bowl: then take soft water enough to cover the yarn or cloth you intend to color, put it into a brass or copper kettle, and bring it nearly to a boiling heat, and just before boiling add 1½ ounces Cream Tartar, boil it a minute or two, then add the Lac and Com.; boil 4 or 5 minutes; then wet the yarn or cloth in water, wring it out and put it into the dye, boil three quarters of an hour; then rinse in clean cold water, and dry in the shade.

Yellow Dye.—Fustic, turmeric powder, barbery-bush, peach leaves, marigold flowers, all make yellow dye. Set the dye with alum; a piece the size of a small nutmeg to each quart of water.

Yellow.—One pound wool or cloth, three-quarters of a pound fustic, quarter pound alum; put all into an earthern vessel, and pour on sufficient hot water to cover the wool, and keep it warm all night; give it half an hour's boil in a brass kettle, and then rinse in cold water. A much deeper and richer yellow may be made by using turmeric powder instead of fustic, and proceeding in the same manner.

Green.—To 1 lb. of yarn or cloth use 2 and a half ounces of alum, and 1 lb. of Fustic; steep to get the strength, but not boil; soak the cloth until a good yellow; throw out the chips; add the Indigo Compound little at a time until a good color.

[1867]　　　THE RECEIPT BOOK.　　　53

HECTOR McLEAN,

AUCTIONEER,

AND

REAL ESTATE AGENT.

OFFICE........No. 19, SOUTH SIDE SPARKS STREET.

Money to Loan on Good Real Estate.

LAND SOLD BY PRIVATE CONTRACT, AND HOUSES RENTED.

Parties at a distance from the Capital will please communicate by letter.

ALL KINDS OF GOODS Sold on REASONABLE TERMS,

And sales spunctually attended to.

Cochineal Scarlet.—For 1 lb. of Wool take water sufficient to cover the yarn, and when lukewarm, add 1¼ oz. Cream Tartar, stir and when the water becomes hot throw in ¼ oz. Cochineal in very fine powder; as the bath begins to boil introduce the yarn, rinse briskly for two or three rotations, and, at the end of two hours, the cloth must be taken out and allowed to become cool, after which, it should be well washed out in pure water; now fill with water until you get the original quantity, and when at the boiling point add 1¼ oz. Cochineal in fine powder; stir, and when the crust which forms on the top has opened in several places 3 oz. mordant must be added, and when the bath has become of a uniform color, the cloth must be put in; rinse briskly, keeping the cloth or yarn under the liquor with a rod, then boil for an hour, then wash in soft water and dry.

Pink.—A pale yet handsome pink may be produced as follows :—One pound of wool, or cloth, half pound good red wood, and quarter pound alum. Soak the wood all night in warm water; add the alum, and boil the cloth in these ingredients for about an hour; take it out and rinse in clean cold water. Or. to 1 lb. of cloth or yarn, use half an ounce Cochineal with one ounce Com. Soak the Cochineal in a brass or copper kettle; then add the Com. and stir; then the cloth, and bring the dye slowly to a scalding heat; vary the time, etc., as above.

Fine Wine Color.—One pound wool, half pound red powder, one ounce madder compound. Soak the powder wood in warm water all night, mix the madder compound with about half a pint of water (in a glass), add to it the rest. Rinse the wool in warm water and put it into the dye; boil about half an hour, take out the wool and rinse in cold water.

1867]   THE RECEIPT BOOK.

BLYTH & KERR,

[Successors to Chas. Garth.]

25, RIDEAU STREET, OTTAWA.

PLUMBERS,

GAS AND STEAM FITTERS,

TIN & COPPER-SMITHS, BELL-HANGERS, &C.

Materials in all the above Branches constantly on hand.

—ALSO—

IMPORTERS AND DEALERS IN

House Furnishing Hardware.

Constantly in Stock:

Cooking Stoves,   Stove Pipes,
Double Stoves,   Sheet Iron,
Hall and Parlor Stoves Galvanized Iron.
Tinware of every description, Churns, Iron Bedsteads,
Baths, Pumps, &c.

Orders from the Country will receive Strict Attention.

Dove and Slate Colors.—Of all shades are made by boiling in an iron vessel, a teacup full of black tea with a teaspoonful of copperas and sufficient water. Dilute this till you get the shade wanted. Sugar paper boiled and set with alum, makes a similar color.

Salmon.—A still richer color, but not hardly so durable may be made in the manner following :—One pound wool, three-quarters of a pound cudbear and a quarter pound alum. Wet the wool and wring it, then boil for about half an hour in a brass kettle and rinse in cold water. A color almost as fine may be had by using quarter pound alum and boiling in the same way.

Salmon Color.— One pound wool, quarter pound anatto, quarter pound soap. Take water sufficient to cover the wool, in which dissolve the anatto and soap ; rinse the wool in warm water, put into the anatto mixture, and boil about half an hour. The shade may be made lighter or deeper to the quantity of anatto used.

Lilac is made by boiling the cloth or wool for a short time in cudbear.

Scouring Liquor.—Cleansing Wool or Cloth from greese, etc., 1 Soft Soap, 1 Sal. Soda, ½ Soda Ash in two gallons of water. The above liquor may also be used for extracting the color from ribbons or other articles you wish to re-color.

Bleaching Liquor.—1 gill muriatic acid, 1 gallon soft water ; soak the wool or cloth for fifteen minutes, and rinse well in pure water.

1867]   THE RECEIPT BOOK.   57

GEORGE COCKER

Has now received and opened out a large and varied stock of

NEW FALL & WINTER GOODS,

COMPRISING

FANCY DRESS GOODS IN GREAT VARIETY,

Aberdeen, Glasgow, Paisley, and Bradford Winceys; Plain and Fancy

Flannels,   Blankets,   Shawls,

Prints,   Cottons,   Tweeds,

OVERCOATINGS, MANTLE CLOTHS,

Hosiery,

Gloves, Lambs Wool Underclothing,

Collars, Neckties, Scarfs, &c. Also, one case Black and Colored French Merinos,

VERY CHEAP.

HOOP SKIRTS, AS USUAL, the CHEAPEST in the CITY

No. 34 SPARKS STREET, CENTRAL TOWN,

OTTAWA.

TOILET RECEIPTS.

Camphorated Dentifrice.—Prepared chalk one pound, camphor two drachms. The camphor must be mixed with a little spirits of wine and finely powdered, and then thoroughly mixed with the chalk.

Wash for the Teeth.—Dissolve two ounces of borax in three pints of water; before it is quite cold add to it one teaspoonful of the tincture of Myrrh and one tablespoonful of the spirit of camphor. To use it mix one wine glassful with half a pint of tepid water. If used daily it arrests decay of the teeth and hardens the gums.

Bears Grease—(Substitute for).—Hogs lard 16 ounces, flowers of benzoin ¼ ounce, palm oil ¼ ounce. Does not easily become rancid. Most nutritious for the hair.

Marrow and Castor Oil Pomatum.—Procure two fresh marrow-bones, and remove the marrow carefully out of them, put it into cold water until it is quite clean; this will take three or four days, during which the water must be frequently changed. Then put the marrow in a clean bowl, dissolve it, and strain it through muslin; after which add four ounces of castor oil. Beat these together with a silver fork until they are almost cold; but before the pomade sets, add the scent—half an ounce, if strong, will be required. This must not be added until cold, or else it evaporates.

Common Pomatum.—Mutton suet one pound, lard three pounds, carefully melted together and stirred constantly while cooling; two ounces of bergamot being added.

Hard Pomatum.—One pound of lard, one pound of mutton suet, four ounces of white wax, one ounce essence of bergamot.

1867] THE RECEIPT BOOK. 59

ANGUS & HUCKELL,

WHOLESALE AND RETAIL

BOOT, SHOE AND LEATHER STORE,

15, SUSSEX STREET,

(WHITE'S BRICK BLOCK,)

Have always on hand the LARGEST and BEST STOCK of

BOOTS,
RUBBERS,
BUCK MOCCASINS, &c.

SHOES,
BUCK MITTS,

A liberal discount given to all Wholesale Buyers.

A. ANGUS. T. HUCKELL.

THE RECEIPT BOOK. [1867

In making Pomatums, the lard, fat, suet or marrow should be carefully prepared by being melted with as gentle a heat as possible, and then skimmed, strained and cleared from all dregs.

An Excellent Hair Wash.—One ounce of borax with half an ounce of camphor, powdered fine, and dissolved in one quart of boiling water. May be used as soon as cool. This is excellent to preserve, beautify and strengthen the hair.

To keep Hair from Falling Out.—Eau de Cologne, two ounces; tincture of cantharadis, two drachmns; oil of lavender, ten drops. This lotion should be used twice a day for some time. If the skin becomes sore, discontinue for a time.

To Prevent Baldness.—Soak one drachm of powdered catharides for a week in one ounce of proof spirits, and mix the tincture with half a pound of beef marrow, carefully melted and strained; add twelve drops of oil of bergamot. Should be used daily.

Bandoline.—Boil one quarter of an ounce of Irish moss in a quart of water until sufficiently thick; add to it a little rectified spirit to prevent it being mildewed. The quantity of spirit will depend on the length of time you desire to keep.

For Freckles.—Take one ounce of lemon juice, one ¼ drachm of powdered borax, and half a drachm of sugar; mix them, and let them stand for a few days in a glass bottle, then rub the liquor on the face and hands occasionally. This will remove them.

To Destroy Offensive Breath.—Six or eight drops of the choloride of soda in a wine-glassful of water. Rinse the mouth well with it.

CHALMERS & CO.,

[Late Beach & Co.,]

DEALERS IN

LAMPS, CHANDELIERS

—AND—

CHIMNEYS.

Canadian and Pennsylvania Rock Oil, Benzine

—AND—

MACHINE OIL

Singers Sewing Machines and Needles,

BERLIN AND all Kinds of FANCY WOOLS,

SMALL WARES, TOYS, &c., &c.

NO. 62, SPARKS STREET

OTTAWA.

To Soften the Skin and Improve the Complexion.—Mix flowers of sulphur with a little milk. After it has stood for an hour or two, rub the milk into the skin. A little of the mixture should be prepared over night for use in the morning. If kept longer it becomes putrid.

Wash for Sunburn.—Take two drachms of borax, one drachm of alum, one drachm of camphor, half an ounce of sugar candy, and a pound of ox gall. Mix and stir well for ten minutes, and repeat the stirring three times a day for a fortnight till it appears clear and transparent. Strain it through blotting paper, and bottle for use.

Honey Soap.—Cut two pounds of yellow soap into thin slices; melt it in a sauce-pan with a little water to prevent it burning. After it has boiled for a few minutes add a quarter of a pound of honey and a like quantity of palm oil, and three pennyworth of the oil of cinnamon; let all boil together for six or eight minutes, then pour it into a pan and let it cool for use.

HINTS TO HOUSEKEEPERS.

To Clean Gold Chains in Two Minutes.—Put the chain into a small glass bottle, with warm water or eau-de-cologne, a little camphorated chalk (tooth-powder); scrape in some soap. Cork the bottle, and shake it for a minute violently. The friction against the glass polishes the gold, and the soap and chalk extract every particle of grease and dirt from the interstices of a chain of the most intricate pattern. On taking it out of the bottle rinse it in clear cold water, wipe it with a towel, and the polish, when all the damp has been allowed to evaporate, will surprise you.

JAMES BUCHANAN,

IMPORTER, AND GENERAL DEALER IN

TEAS, COFFEES, WINES, LIQUORS,

AND CHOICE GROCERIES,

Sussex Street, Lower Town, and Wellington Street, Upper Town.

———o———

AGENT for McEWAN'S CELEBRATED PORTLAND FINNAN HADDIES

COFFEE

Roasted and Ground daily on the premises, by Steam Power, consequently always to be had in the highest state of perfection.

To Remove Ink Stains from Silver.—The tops and other portions of silver inkstands frequently become discolored with ink which it is difficult to remove. It may, however, be eradicated by making a little choloride of lime into paste and rubbing it upon the stains.

To Clean Silks, Satins or Colored Woolen Dresses.—Four ounces soft soap, four ounces of honey, the white of one egg, and one wineglass of gin; mix well together, afterwards rinse the article in cold water and let drain. Iron while damp.

To Remove Wax Spots from Cloth.—Hold a piece of red hot iron within an inch or two of the marks, afterwards rub them with a clean soft rag.

Scouring drops for Removing Grease Spots.—Camphene or spirits of turpentine—three ounces; essence of lemon one ounce; mix well.

Fruit or wine stains that have been long in linen may be removed by rubbing the part on each side with yellow soap. Then lay on a mixture of starch very thick; rub it well in, and expose the linen to the sun and air till the stain comes out, which will be in three or four days.

Oil-cloth should never be scrubbed, but after it is swept it should be washed with a soft cloth and lukewarm water. Soap or hot water are sure to injure the paint.

To clean paint, smear a piece of flannel in common whiting, mixed to the consistency of common paste, in warm water. Rub the surface to be cleansed quite briskly, and wash off with pure cold water. Grease spots will in this way be almost instantly removed, as well as other filth, and the paint will retain its brilliancy and beauty unimpaired.

[1867]   THE RECEIPT BOOK.   65

THE BEST ASSORTMENT OF

Fancy & Staple Dry Goods

in this city, to be found at

CUNNINGHAM & LINDSAY'S,

14 RIDEAU STREET, OTTAWA.

C

THE RECEIPT BOOK. [1867

Mildewed linen may be cleaned by soaping the spots while wet, covering them with fine chalk scraped to powder, and well rubbed in.

To Clean Wall Paper.—Blow the dust carefully off the walls with a bellows, and gently rub the paper with stale bread. Cut the surface from the bread as soon as it is dirty. Great caution should be used not to rub the paper too hard, nor to rub it cross ways. If carefully done it will make old paper look almost as good as new.

Papier-Mache should be cleaned with a sponge and cold water without soap; dredged with flour while damp, and polished with flannel.

To Clean Bronzed Lamps.—Bronzed lamps should be dusted daily with a feather, brush, or soft cloth, as washing them is apt to destroy the bronzing.

To Clean Looking-Glasses.—Wash the glass with lukewarm soap-suds and a sponge; when dry rub it well with a piece of buckskin and some finely powdered chalk.

To Clean Japanned Trays.—Wash with a sponge and cold water, and rub dry with a soft cloth. Warm water and soap will injure the appearance of the articles.

To Clean Silverware.—Wash the articles daily with a sponge and soap-suds, and wipe them dry with a soft towel.

To clean straw matting use a large cloth, and salt and water, and wipe quite dry. The salt preserves the color of the mattings, and prevents it turning yellow.

Cement for Broken China or Glass.— Dissolve half an ounce of gum accurcia in a wineglass of boiling water. Add plaster of Paris enough to form a thick paste; apply it with a brush to the parts required to be cemented together.

1867]   THE RECEIPT BOOK.   67

RIDEAU STREET.   **RIDEAU STREET.**
No. 10,   No. 10,

HOWE'S
BOOT, SHOE, AND TRUNK STORE.

THIS ESTABLISHMENT is one of the OLDEST in the City of Ottawa, and still retains its reputation as being reliable for everything in the Line of FEET WEAR.

The Stock is supplied from the best Manufacturing Houses in Canada, and can, therefore,

BE WARRANTED AS REPRESENTED.

A continuance of a proportionate share of the Public Patronage is respectfully solicited.

GEO. HOWE & SON.

Brown Holland Chair-Covers.—After being washed clean in the usual manner, they must be rinsed at the last in water in which some hay has been boiled. This will restore the color which has been washed out, and they will have the appearance of being new. This is also a good plan for the brown-white crumb-cloths and coverings for stair-carpets.

To Renovate Black Silk.—Rub the sil allk over on the right side with a solution of ammonia and water (two teaspoonfuls of powdered ammonia to a quarter of a pint of warm water,) and smooth it on the wrong side with a moderately hot iron, and the silk will regain a bright black appearance.

Improvement in Starching.—Take two ounces of white gumarabic powder, put it into a pitcher, and pour on it a pint or more of boiling water (according to the degree of strength required), and then, having covered it, let it stand all night. The next day, pour it carefully from the dregs into a clean bottle, cork it, and keep it for use. A tablespoonful of this gum-water, stirred into a pint of starch that has been made in the usual manner, will give lawns (either white, black, or printed) a look of newness when nothing else can restore them after washing. It is also good, much diluted, for thin white muslin and bobbinet.

To Wash Kid Gloves.—Have ready a little new milk in one saucer and a piece of brown soap in another, and a clean towel folded three or four times. Spread the glove out neatly on the cloth. Dip a piece of flannel in the milk and rub a quantity of the soap on it. With the soaped and wetted flannel rub the glove downwards towards the fingers till the glove looks a dingy-yellow—if white. Let it dry and it will look almost like new.

HARDWARE!

ALEX. WORKMAN & CO.,

Hardware Merchants,

AND MANUFACTURERS' AGENTS.

WAREHOUSES:—Rideau street and Canal Basin, Lower Town; and Wellington street, Upper Town. Keep constantly on hand every variety of

SHELF and HEAVY HARDWARE,

Including Bar, Bundle and Sheet Iron, Canada Plates, Tin, Galvanized and Russia Sheet Iron, Nails, Glass, Putty, Chain Anchors, &c.

Agents for the Goods manufactured by Messrs. FROTHINGHAM & WORKMAN, at Cote St. Paul Works, Montreal, consisting of Augers, Axes, Scythes, Shovels, Spades, Cut and Horse-Shoe Nails, &c. &c.,

I. & J. TAYLOR'S Patent Fire Proof Safes,

THURBER'S Patent Anti-Friction Metal,

HAMILTON POWDER COMPANY,

McNELLY & SONS' Church and other Bells,

E. & C. GUNNEY'S Patent Platform Scales.

Box and Cooking Stoves, Grates, &c., &c.

Nettle Stings.—Nettle stings may be cured by rubbing the part with mint or sage leaves.

A Cure for burns and scalds.—Four ounces of powdered alum put into a pint of cold water. A piece of rag kept wet with this should be applied to the burn or scald, and it will be rapidly cured.

To Preserve furs from Moth.—In one pint of warm water dissolve twelve grains of corrosive sublimate. If washed with this and dried, no moths will attack the furs. This mixture should be marked POISON.

Lamp Wicks.—If lamp wicks are soaked in strong vinager and well dried there is little danger of a lamp smoking.

Stair carpets should always have a slip of paper put under them, at and over the edge of every stair, which is the part where they first wear out, in order to lessen the friction of the carpets against the boards beneath. The strips should be within an inch or two as long as the carpet is wide, and about four or five inches in breadth, so as to be a distance from each stair. This simple plan, so easy of execution, will, we know, preserve a stair carpet half as long again as it would last without the strips of paper.

To Prevent the Nails Growing Down into the Toes.—This is a very troublesome, and sometimes dangerous thing, for I know an instance of toes having to be amputed in consequence. But the cure is very simple. Take a sharp-pointed knife, and cut a little furrow all along the top of the nail lengthwise. As it fills up scrape it out again. This will cause the nail to contract at the top, and so loosen its hold from the flesh. Persevere until the difficulty is entirely overcome.

… THE RECEIPT BOOK.

KEARNS & RYAN,

DRY GOODS MERCHANTS,

UNION BLOCK,

CORNER OF YORK AND SUSSEX STREETS,

OTTAWA.

———o———

THE above firm keep constantly on hand a large assortment of the following Goods:—

Canadian Tweeds from the best factories in Canada.
Canadian, American and English Grey Cottons.
Canadian, American and Southern Cotton yarn.
Prints and Shirtings—best and cheapest in the trade.
Dress Goods—well assorted and low figures.
Black Broad Cloths and Mantle Cloths, extra good value.
Flannels (plain and Fancy) to suit all tastes.
Hosiery and Gloves (plain and fancy), &c., &c., &c.

☞ They have also opened out a new Show Room, in which they are prepared to show

BONNETS AND HATS, Trimmed and untrimmed.
    MANTLES,
        SHAWLS,
            HOOP-SKIRTS,
                LACE CURTAINS, &c.,

And all at such prices as must give satisfaction.

⁎ Orders for Bonnets, Mantles and Dresses strictly attended to.

Please remember the House—Corner of York and Sussex streets.

Frost Bites.—If frost-bitten be careful not to expose the injured parts to heat from a fire. The best remedy is simple friction with the hand, or a piece of COLD flannel.

Cure for Corns.—One teaspoonful of tar, one of coarse brown sugar, and one of saltpetre. The whole to be warmed together. Spread it on kid leather the size of the corns, and in two days they will be drawn out.

Apoplexy.—Cattle attacked with this disease are generally in a plethoric condition. The usual indications are COINA (a sleepy state) eyes protruding, short quick breathing. In such cases bleeding should be resorted to at once; give in drink one pound of epsom salts.

A Sure Cure for Corns.—Strong Acetic acid applied night and morning with a camels hair brush. In about a week the corn will have disappeared.

DISEASES OF CATTLE AND THEIR REMEDIES.

Worms on the Bronchial Tubes.—Symptoms: a rough starring coat—hide bound; painful cough, respiration hurried. Little can be done for this; but small doses of spirits of turpentine are sometimes successful.

Worms.—Cattle are not subject to worms as are other domestic animals. Where they do exist they are readily driven out by doses of sulphate of iron—one half drachm twice a day given in molasses.

Ulcers about the Joints.—At times the joints assume an ulcerated appearance. Apply one part of alum to two parts of prepared chalk powder, and sprinkle on the ulcerated parts.

FINGLAND & DRAPER

(BROUGH'S OLD STAND, SUSSEX STREET),

IMPORTERS OF

STAPLE AND FANCY DRY GOODS,

Have always on hand an extensive, well assorted and cheap stock of

Dress Goods, French Merinoes,

Delaines, Lustres, Cobourgs,

Skirtings, Winceys, Flannels,

Mantle Cloths, &c.

THE RECEIPT BOOK. 1867

Red Water—so called from the color of the urine voided by the animal. Respiration hurried, high fever, rumination ceases, animal moans, arches its back, and strains in passing urine, which is deeply tinged with blood. The disease is caused in general from feeding on turnips grown on ill-drained land. Give one pint of linseed oil. Clysters of soap may be freely used. Give plenty of linseed tea. If urine is abundant give one ounce tincture of opiun and one drachm of powdered alloes three times, at intervals of eight hours.

Milk fever produces shaking in hind legs, a staggering gait, pulse from sixty to eighty, moaning, set eyes, general stupor and slow respiration. Give Epsom salts—one pound; ginger—two ounces; dissolve in one quart of water. Rub the back and loins well with three ounces of strong mustard, amonia and water—each one ounce and a half. Never bleed for this disease.

Pneumonia—Generally caused by sudden cold to an overheated animal, causing a determination of blood to the lungs, and causing death by suffocation. The disease is generally preceded by shivering dry skin, clamy mouth, short cough. Treatment : Bleed freely and give in drench one pound of Glauber salts with two drachms of ginger.

Mad Staggers.—The active symptoms are generally preceeded by stupor. The animal becomes stubborn, eyes full and red, respiration rapid, delerium soon succeeds ; the animal dashes about, bent on mischief. Caused by overwork in warm weather and too stimulating food. Bleed almost to fainting should be resorted to at the early stage, followed by a brisk purge—say one pound of Epsom salt. Broken ice applied to the head is very useful. Rub along the spine with mustard, hartshorn and water.

ESTABLISHED 1848!

P. A. EGLESON & SON,

GENERAL FAMILY GROCERS

AND

PROVISION MERCHANTS,

No. 80 SUSSEX STREET, OTTAWA,

DEALERS IN

Fine TEAS, SUGARS, COFFEES,

SPICES, TOBACCOS, &c., &c.

FINEST BRANDS OF

PORK, HERRINGS, and TABLE CODFISH.

Also, always on hand,

Best American Cotton Yarns, Warranted,

Weavers' Reeds, Shuttles, Harness, and General Supplies.

GIVE THEM A CALL.

Thrush in the Mouth.—This disease yields readily to proper treatment. Three ounces of epsom salts should be given once a day for three or four days. Wash the mouth well with a solution of alum, or vinager and honey. The disease will disappear in a few days.

Gut-tie is of rare occurrence. When it sets in no relief can be afforded, and the poor brute must suffer till it dies.

Rheumatism caused by exposure to wet and cold. Symptoms : loss of appetite, stiff joints, nose dry, coat starring, joints sometimes swollen. Mild purgatives should be used ; half ounce doses of colchium root in powder, or ounce balls of pine tar. As a local application Kerosene oil, well rubbed in, is very useful.

Joint Murrain—Known also as quarter evil and black quarter—common among young cattle, and often fatal. The joints become suddenly swollen and painful, producing lameness, general feverishness and tenderness in loins, the head poked out, breath and roots of horns hot, muzzle dry, nostrils expanded, pulse feel hard and rapid. Bleed at once, and give active purgatives ; afterwards give one of the following powders every half hour. Nitrate of Potassa—two ounces ; tartrate of antimony and pulverized degitalis—one and a half drachms each; mix and divide into eight powders. Give cold linseed tea plentifully.

Hydrophobia.—An animal attacked with this is incurable ; and the sooner it is destroyed the better. Should it bite another animals let 'the wound be searched for and freely opened with a knife, and lunar caustic, or caustic potash at once applied to all parts, not allowing the slightest scratch to escape. If attended to in time this will save the animal.

OTTAWA
MUSIC AND Fancy Goods STORE,
25 SPARKS STREET.

J. L. ORME & SON,

IMPORTERS OF

Piano-Fortes, Melodeons, Voilins, Guitars, Concertinas, Violin and Guitar Strings, Sheet Music, and Books.

FANCY GOODS, BERLIN WOOLS,

Cricketing and Archery Goods, Toys, &c., &c.

N. B.—Music sent by Mail on receipt of the marked price, Post Free.

PIANOS TUNED AND REPAIRED.

25 SPARKS STREET, opposite Garland, Mutchmor & Co's.

Garget—A hard knotty condition of the udder, which sometimes follows calving, in consequence of the sudden distention of the bag with milk. Let the calf suck the dam as speedily as possible, if the hardness is not then removed foment the udder with warm water. Wipe it dry and anoint it with melted lard as hot as the animal will bear. The most obstinate cases will yield to this treatment. If abscesses form they should be lanced.

Cow Pox—Appears in the form of an eruption on the teats of the cow. Treatment.—Foment the teats with warm water and castile soap, afterwards wipe the bag dry and dress it with citerine ointment.

Diarrhœa.—Cattle are frequently subject to this disease in the spring when the grass is young and soft. The symptoms are too well known to require description. If the attack is mild the diet is low—give two ounces of Epsom salts twice a day. In more obstinate cases give two drachms of carbonate of soda in the food.

Clue Bound.—This is caused by the third stomach being choked with dry, hard food. The animal eats voraciously for a while and stops suddenly trembling—the countenance becomes haggard, the eye wild, and foaming takes place at the mouth. One quart of potash dissolved in water, given three times a day, is most ufeful in this disease.

Hoove—or blown is the result of fermentation in the paunch caused by the animal having eaten too freely of wet grass, luxuriant clover, turnips, &c., which causes much pain to the animal and threatens suffocation. Injections of soap and water should be freely used. If the case seems very bad the paunch should be punctured. The proper point to operate upon is midway between the last rib and the hip bone, about twelve inches from the centre of the back or loins.

FINGLAND & DRAPER,

IMPORTERS OF

PRINTS, GREY AND WHITE COTTONS,

HOSIERY, GLOVES, TIES, FEATHERS, FLOWERS,

BROAD-CLOTHS, COATINGS,

Tweeds, Canada Cloths,
Grey Lumbering Blankets,
White Lumbering Blankets,

BEST COTTON WARPS.

ASSORTED NUMBERS AND COLORS.

Mange.—A contagious disease, mainly caused by poor food and want of cleanlinesss. The animal should be kept away from all others and well washed with castile soap and water. When dried, apply with a scrubbing brush the following mixture—white hellabore, one ounce; sulphur flower, three ounces; gas water, one quart; mix all well together. Give internally one of the following powders in the feed night and morning. Flowers of sulphur one ounce, black antimony one ounce, nitrate of potassa one ounce, mix and divide into eight powders.

Foul in the foot—Caused by hard substances getting between the claws, producing inflammation and ulceration of the parts, the pasterns swell and the animal becomes lame. The foot should be well washed and the foreign substances removed. A piece of tow saturated with tar and sprinkled with sulphate of copper should be placed between the claws. This usually requires but one or two applications.

Lice.—Cattle are very subject to lice when neglected and poorly fed. Good feeding and the treatment prescribed for mange is what they require to cure them.

Open Joints—Generally the result of an accident—causes considerable nervous irritation and lock-jaw. Close the wound as soon as possible and apply collodion. Shoemaker's wax will answer very well at times.

Rupture of the bladder sometimes takes place.—There are no symptoms by which it is known nor any cure for it. It always proves fatal.

Worms on the brain.—This occasionally occurs. Spmptoms: loss of appetite, suspended rumination, horns and ears hot, respiration disturbed, coat dry. No course of treatment will prove beneficial in this disease.

THE NEW DOMINION
DRY GOODS
—— AND ——
READY MADE CLOTHING

ESTABLISHMENT,

☞ NO. 47, SUSSEX STREET,

Union Block, next to the Tea Pot,

OTTAWA.

☞ Every article in his line of business kept constantly on hand, superior in quality and moderate in price.

JAMES HIGGINSON, Proprietor.

Hoose.—This disease frequently arises from the impure air of crowded cow houses. Scanty and poor provender will also produce it. The symptoms are: loss of appetite, muzzle dry, coat rough, respiration quickened, horns hot, ears, nose and legs cold, husky cough, frequently constipated. Treatment: Alloes—one and a half ounces; Nitrate of potassia—half an ounce; ginger—six drachms; mix and divide into six powders. Give one every six hours till the bowels are opened.

Inflammation of the Haw.—Apply to the eye a wash of rain water, one pint; in which mix one ounce of tincture of opium.

Inflammation of the bladder—Generally accompanied with inflammation of the kidneys. The pulse is full and rapid, mouth clammy, nose dry, eyes bloodshot, appetite lost, moaning and walks with a staggering gait, frequent efforts to pass urine in small quantities. Inject one quart of tepid water with an ounce and a half of opium. Give internally one of the following powders every hour until relieved. Nitrate of potassa one ounce, tatrate of antimony and pulverized degitales leaves, one drachm each, mix and divide into six powders.

Wood Evil, caused by eating buds of young oak, ash, or other trees, of a highly stimulating nature. Symptoms are: loss of appetite, suspended rumination, mouth hot, skin dry, pulse from sixty to seventy, swelling and pain in the belly, obstinate constipation, urine of strong odour and highly colored. The animal should be bled, and a strong purgative given. Injections of castile soap and water should be freely used. The application of mustard, hartshorn and water to the belly will be found beneficial.

[1867] THE RECEIPT BOOK.

SMITH & RODNEY,

MERCHANT TAILORS,

AND

GENERAL OUTFITTERS,

DIRECTLY OPPOSITE THE MAIN ENTRANCE TO THE RUSSELL HOUSE, ON ELGIN STREET.

A good assortment of ENGLISH, FRENCH, and GERMAN CLOTHS constantly on hand; Vestings of all varieties. A large stock of

CANADIAN TWEEDS,

from the best manufacturers in the Province; also a perfect stock of

Ready-Made Clothing.

Particular attention paid to the Custom Department. All garments warranted to suit the purchaser's order, as the proprietors are first-class cutters.

B. B. RODNEY.   THOMAS SMITH.

Navel ill.—Inflammation of the navel occurs at times with calves, causing redness and pain. If not promptly looked to will carry the creature off. Foment the part well with warm hop tea, after which apply a cloth saturated with lead water and secured by bandages. Give internally doses of Epsom salts, two ounces in half-a-pint of water.

Inflamation of the liver, known as the yellows, or gaundice. Symptoms : a yellow color in the eye, soreness on pressure of right side, loss of appetite, dulness, constipation, urine highly colored. Calomel is the best remedy known, but been so abused as to fall into disrepute. Give Epsom salts nightly in four ounce doses, with one scruple of Calomel until the animal is relieved. Mustard and water should be applied to the right side, and well rubbed in.

Inflamation of the Kidneys.—Loins tender, urine voided in small quantities. The animal becomes dull and feeds daintily, urine highly colored and bloody, nose dry, horns, ears and legs cold, respiration hurried, pulse full, hard and throbbing. Give one pint of linseed oil and ten drops of castor oil mixed together, follow this with small doses of salts once a day. Give injections of water—one half gallon to two ounces tincture of arnica. Mustard applications to the loins are very useful.

DISEASES OF SHEEP AND THEIR REMEDIES.

Sore Mouth.—The lips of sheep sometimes become suddenly sore, and swell to the thickness of a man's hand. The malady occasionally attacks whole flocks and becomes fatal. It is usually brought on by noxious weeds, interspersed among the hay. To cure it—daub the lips well with tar.

1867]   THE RECEIPT BOOK.   85

The Two Highest Premiums,
AND
ONLY GOLD MEDALS
FOR SEWING MACHINES, AT THE
Paris Exhibition of 1867,
Were awarded to the

Wheeler & Wilson Manufacturing Company, and the Howe Machine Company, both of New York.

The WHEELER & WILSON is crowned with the unparalleled number of **65 Medals**, and stands to-day, as it has stood for years, WITHOUT A RIVAL **FOR FAMILY USE**, RAPID TAILORING, etc., etc.

LONDON, 1862. PARIS, 1861.

The new Button Hole Attachment for this Machine is now ready. It is the greatest invention of the day. Also, Embroidering Attachments, and other latest improvements.

THE HOWE MACHINES ARE WORLD RENOWNED
for doing the handsomest and most durable leather work.

They are the best Shuttle Machine for Tailors' use.

The **NEW HOWE FAMILY MACHINE** is a charming Machine.

G. A. WALTON, Agent, 37 Sparks St., Ottawa.
Spool Silk, Spool Cotton, Needles, Oil, etc., etc.

Maggots.—Rams, with horns growing close to their heads are liable to have maggots generated under them, particularly if the skin on the surrounding parts is broken with fighting, and unless removed soon destroy the animal. Boiled tar is both a preventive and remedy. If put under the horns when the sheep are marked, no trouble will arise from them.

Maggot Flies.—Sometimes flies deposit their eggs on the backs of open wooled sheep and the young insects will tease the animal, causing fever, and, at times, death. Tar and turpentine, or butter and sulphur smeared over the parts are admirable preventitives.

Pelt rot arises from hard keeping and exposure to cold and wet. The wool falls off and leaves the sheep nearly naked, and a reddish crust appears on the skin. The remedy is full feeding and a warm stall, anointing the hard parts of the skin with tar, oil and butter.

Palsy.—In winter, poor lambs, or feeble ewes in the spring occasionally loose the power of walking or standing. Warmth, gentle stimulants and good nursery may restore it, but in general, it is as well to destroy its life at once.

Inflamation of the Eyes.—This will generally disappear of itself in a few days. To ease the animal a little blood may be drawn from under the eyes, which should then be bathed in tepid water, and occasionally with a weak solution of sulpate of zinc and opium.

Caked bag, or garget, is inflammation of the udder, generally caused by too great an accumulation of milk prior to lambing, or in consequence of the death of the lamb. The milk should be drained a few times at increasing intervals, washing the fur sometimes in cold water at each milking. If there is fever with it give an ounce of Epsom salts.

THE MARKET DRUG STORE,

(OPPOSITE HAMILTON'S HOTEL)

YORK STREET - - - OTTAWA.

The above store is now open with a new and complete assortment of

PURE DRUGS,

CHEMICALS, GENUINE PATENT MEDICINES.

DYE STUFFS, PERFUMERY,

BRUSHES, COMBS, and TOILET ARTICLES,

BRILLIANT CANADA ROCK OIL,

Will burn longer, and is much lower in price than Pennsylvania.

COAL OIL LAMPS

Of all descriptions.

PAINTS, OILS, VARNISHES, &C., &C.

SPECTACLES

To suit all sights.

TELESCOPES, MICROSCOPES, and all descriptions of OPTICAL INSTRUMENTS.

WM. HEARN.

Sore Face.—Sheep feeding on pastures infested with certain weeds exhibit an irritation of skin about the nose and face, and lose the hair about those parts. The irritation sometimes extends over the whole body. If these plants are eaten in large quantities they produce violent inflammation of the bowels which is often fatal. The irritated parts should be rubbed with a mixture of lard and sulphur. If inflammation sets in put a little into the sheep's mouth with a flattened stick. Abundance of salt is a good preventative.

Fractures.—If the bone simply is broken and no wound to the soft parts, apply a piece of wet leather, taking care to ease the limb when swelling comes on. If the swelling is considerable bleed the animal. Give Epsom salts in ounce doses. If the bones are kept steady they will reunite in three or four weeks—more quickly in young sheep than old ones. Should the soft parts be greatly injured recovery is very uncertain, and it becomes a question if it is not better to slaughter the animal at once.

Costiveness.—This may be overcome by giving two table-spoonfulls of castor oil every twelve hours until the trouble ceases, or give instead one ounce of Epsom salts.

Diarrhœa.—Generally brought on by eating improper food, such as bad hay or noxious weeds, or by a sudden change of food. It is important to distinguish this disease from dysentery. In diarrhœa there is no apparent fever and the appetite remains good. Confinement to dry food will often check it. To a lamb give half an ounce of Epsom salts, followed by an astringent; or give half a drachm of rhubarb, or an ounce of linseed tea. Give once a day an ounce of prepared chalk in half a pint of tepid milk for two or three days.

1867] THE RECEIPT BOOK. 89

JAMES HOPE & Co.,
Manufacturing Stationers,

BOOK BINDERS,

AND IMPORTERS OF

GENERAL STATIONERY,

ARTISTS' MATERIALS,

SCHOOL BOOKS,

BIBLES, CHURCH SERVICES, PRAYER BOOKS, HYMN BOOKS, PHOTOGRAPHIC ALBUMS, &c., &c.

———o———

Particular attention given to the manufacture of

BLANK BOOKS,

Of the best material and workmanship.

———o———

BOOKBINDING AND PAPER RULING

In all their branches, executed in the best style, and with dispatch.

Corner of Sparks and Elgin Streets,

JAMES HOPE.
S. S. M. HUNTER.

OTTAWA.

Snuffles—The best course is to prevent this disease by good, well ventilated shelter, with a sufficiency of food regularly administered.

Colic, commonly called "stretches."—Sheep are sometimes seen lying down and rising every moment or two, constantly stretching their fore and hind legs far apart, appear in pain and refuse food. This results from flatulent colic. Give the animal half an ounce of Epsom salts, a drachm of Jamaica Ginger, and sixty drops of essence of peppermint. The salts alone will often effect a cure.

Bronchitis.—The symptoms are those of an ordinary cold, but attended with more fever and tenderness of the throat and belly when pressed. Administer salt in doses of about one and a half ounces, and seven ounces of lime water given at another part of the day.

Braxy—Is most common in late autumn and spring. Entire prevention may be secured by warm, dry shelter and nutritious food. The animal becomes uneasy, neglects its food, drinks frequently, the belly becomes swollen and the back drawn up. Remedies should be promptly applied. Bleed freely. To effect this it may be necessary to place the sheep in hot water as the blood is stagnant. Give two ounces of Epsom salts and a handful of common salt in warm water. Bed the animal in dry straw and cover with a blanket.

Appoplexy—Destroys a sheep in a few minutes. The animal leaps frantically in the air, dashes itself on the ground and soon dies. Bleeding should at once be resorted to, and till the pulse is lowered and the muscles relax. If the animal is a strong one two ounces of Epsom salts may at once be given to it. If this fails to open the bowels, give half an ounce of salts twice a day.

W. M. MASSEY,

IMPORTER OF

GENUINE DRUGS AND CHEMICALS,

PERFUMERY and TOILET REQUISITES,

PATENT MEDICINES, SPICES

SEEDS, DYE STUFFS, &c.,

MEDICAL HALL,

28 SPARKS STREET, OTTAWA CITY.

Administering medicine.—The stomach into which medicines are to be administered is the fourth or digesting stomach. The comparatively insensible coatings of the paunch are but slightly acted on except by doses of improper magnitude. Medicine to reach the fourth stomach should be given in as fluid a form as possible, and should be drunk slowly and not gulped rapidly or forcibly down the throat.

Feeling the pulse.—The number of pulsations can be determined by feeling the heart beat on the left side. The pulsations in a healthy full grown sheep should be from sixty-five to seventy.

Bleeding.—The good effects of bleeding depend almost as much on the rapidity with which blood is extracted as on the quantity taken. Bleed rapidly or not at all. The amount of blood drawn should depend on the constitutional effects not by measurement. Caution must be exercised in this respect as many animals are destroyed by bleeding in disorders not requiring it.

Fouls.—Sheep encounter this disease if kept in filthy yards or on very moist ground. It is an irritation of the cleft of the foot, producing lameness and resembles "hoof ail" in appearance. A little solution of blue vitriol, followed by a coating of warm tar promptly cures it. For foul noses—dip a small swab in tar, then roll it in salt, smear some on the nose and compel the sheep to swallow a little.

THE DISEASES OF THE HORSE AND THEIR REMEDIES.

Fits.—You had better, in this case, send for the surgeon at once, if your horse be valuable; if otherwise, get rid of him.

D. R. LEAVENS,

WHOLESALE AND RETAIL DEALER IN

ROCK AND KEROSINE OIL,

Lamps, Chimneys, Wicks, Burning Fluid,

MACHINE OIL, BENZOLE,

73 Sussex Street, Ottawa.

SIGN,—RED BARREL.

Lameness.—It is sometimes difficult to detect the cause of lameness, especially of the anterior extremities; I would, however, say that it is a safe criterion to watch how the horse moves. If he lift his feet, the shoulder is not the injured part; but if the shoulder be affected, the pain that any raising of the foot will occasion will cause him to drag the toe along the ground, instead of attempting to raise the foot. In shoulder-lameness you can do nothing but get the surgeon as soon as possible. In the other case, examine the foot, as found nail or bad shoeing may be the exciting cause.

Stabs or Cuts.—Let your first care be to remove the cause, if any such remain in the wound. Send at the same time for the nearest veterinary surgeon. If there be much effusion of blood, strive to check it as much as possible, while waiting that gentleman's arrival. This may be best done by producing pressure on the bleeding vessels, and effusion of cold water. In some cases a solution of alum, or any other harmless astringent, may be useful. If the bleeding has ceased, commence a continuous and vigorous fomentation. Its alleviates pain, arrests febrile symptoms, and brings the wound into a suppurative state. The very worst wound may often be cured by this simple treatment, instead of hot oils and violent stimulants, which kill more horses than they cure. Pricks in the sole are a very frequent cause of Quittor, and should, therefore, be timely looked to; but observe the manner in which the farrier removes the shoe for the purpose of examination. Do not suffer him to take it off violently. Each nail should be separately extracted, and the shoe then removed; otherwise the affair will probably be made worse. When the shoe is thus gently removed, the appearance of matter or moisture on some particular spot will usually indicate the seat of pain.

WILLIAM WALL,

DEALER IN

Wines, Brandies, Liquors and Choice English and Foreign Groceries

OF ALL KINDS.

NO. 73, RIDEAU, CORNER OF NICHOLAS STREET,

Amongst which may be found

Choice Black, Green and Japan Teas, Porto Rico Cuba and Refined Sugars; Rio, Java and Mocha Mixture, and other Coffees; Solace, Fig, Dark and Bright Half-Pounds, and Old Virginia Tobaccos; Nuts and Fruits of all kinds

---

My stock of LIQUORS is well assorted, and comprises fine Old Ports, Pale and Golden Sherries in Wood and Bottle, fine old Cognac Brandies, Gin, Rum, Scotch and Irish Whiskey, High Wines, Old Rye and Family Proof Whiskies.

Brunell's Round and Labrador Split Herrings, Table Codfish, Mackerel, White Fish and Digby Herrings, in large and small boxes; Liverpool and Fine Salt; Pork, &c.

LABATT'S CELEBRATED ALE

Always on hand, on draft or bottled.

Accidents.—There are also some accidents which the proprietor of a horse may himself with safety look after. For instance, broken knees. When a horse falls and lacerates his knees, your first object should be, by careful washing, to remove all foreign substances from the wound, In the next place, endeavor to ascertain whether the joint cavity has been penetrated. You must not use a probe for this purpose; but apply a poultice of linseed meal,—and when, in about eight or ten hours afterwards, you take it off, you will see a yellowish, glairy fluid effused upon it, if the joints have been penetrated. Should this have been the case, send at once for the veterinary surgeon. When the joint has not been penetrated, get the lips of the wound together, and keep them so by a compress and bandages, which need not be renewed till the third day. The earlier the wound is closed the less mark will be left on the part.

Colic attacks a horse in many instances very suddenly, and requires immediate relief. Send for the veterinary surgeon; but, pending his arrival, give, as a drench, about two ounces of oil of turpentine with six drachms of laudanum,, in a pint of castor or linseed oil, warm. After the spasms have disappeared, rub the horse dry, the belly and flanks especially. I should not, however, recommend the horse to be trotted about, as some do. It is better to let him rest. Give no spirits, pepper, or other stimulants. There are often sad mistakes made in giving the cholic drink to horses suffering from indigestion, or a tendency to inflammation of the bowels. The one is a simple attack, which it is desirable to meet at once; the other a gradual undermining of the vital powers, which a veterinary surgeon alone can cope with. Now the medicine for the one is poison to the other. Hence it is important to discriminate between the symptoms.

1867] THE RECEIPT BOOK. 97

A BEAUTIFUL RECEIPT!

NECESSARY FOR ALL AGES,

And without which, in these extreme latitudes of cold and heat, none are safe. Very soon the toes will be frost bitten, or your toes will be trod upon ; and then how bad it looks without Boots, or with bad ones.

THE REMEDY IS TO BE FOUND AT

OFFORD'S

WHOLESALE AND RETAIL

BOOT AND SHOE STORE

No. 13 RIDEAU STREET, opposite Sussex Street.

Doses necessary to afford Immediate Relief.—Heavy for our Farming Friends and all Men; a little Lighter for our Lady Friends, and Smaller for all Children.

To our numerous friends and to the public we would say : We have goods suited to the Season, to the Feet, and to the Pocket.

OFFORD.

THE RECEIPT BOOK. [1867

Glanders.—In purchasing a horse, be very careful to ascertain that he is unaffected with this truly terribel disease, for which there is no cure, and which has, in so many frightful instances, been communicated both to man and other animals. Notwithstanding the awful nature of this disease, however—not a whit less dreadful than hydrophobia—dealers at fairs and other places will frequently endeavor to pass off a glandered horse upon an unwary customer.

Farcy and Glanders are, to a considerable extent, connected; as each, when neglected, or proving obstinate, is apt to run into the other. Like glanders, farcy is highly contagious, but is not, like that disease, wholly impregnable to the attacks of science. When the disease first appears—and its appearance is familiar to all about horses—give an aperient drench. If it be the button-farcy, touch the buttons with the extremity of a hot iron. If you have no building iron by you, the top of an Italian iron, such as laundresses use, may be made to answer. Examine the sores daily, and as soon as they begin to slough, touch with a solution of a drachm of corrosive sublimate, in an ounce of spirit of wine, to which is added two drachms of creosote. Give internally a ball daily, composed of corrosive sublimate, twelve grains, two drachms of powdered gentian, one drachm of ginger, and one ounce of powdered brimstone. As soon as the mouth begins to look affected by the mercury, or the animal is violently purged, omit the corrosive sublimate, but continue the remainder of the ball. Keep the animal in an airy situation, but one not exposed to draughts or damp, and feed on green meat, such as parsnips and carrots especially. These roots posses sweetening of a high order.

Lampas, or swelling of the bars, or vacant space between the tusks and grinders—an affection very com-

S. ROGERS,
CABINET-MAKER, UPHOLSTERER,
AND UNDERTAKER,
RIDEAU AND GEORGE STREETS, OTTAWA.

---o---

FANCY CHAIRS, OTTOMANS,
AND FIRE SCREENS,
Made to suit Needlework.

---o---

SOFA, COUCH AND CHAIR BEDS
TO ORDER.

---o---

Feather, Hair and Spring Beds, Palliasses, &c.,
MADE TO ORDER.

Carpets laid, Window Drapery fitted up, Cornices and Poles to order. Repairing done at gentlemen's houses; Second-hand Furniture taken in exchange for new

Gentlemen furnishing their own Drawings can have all kinds of Antique Furniture made, or any other article that is made of wood.

Carving, Twisting, and Turning to order; all kinds of House Finishing made; Pictures framed in every style of the art; Winter Sashes removed; Blinds put up, and Joiner's Work of every description executed.

Furniture carefully packed and removed to any part of the City or Province.

Glass, China, and other valuables carefully packed; Packing Boxes made, &c.

N. B.—S. R. has twice superintended the Packing of the Government Furniture for Messrs. Jacques & Hay, of Toronto.

mon to young horses when teething—will generally yield to mild alteratives and cooling drinks; but if it do not, a few slight incisions with a lancet or penknife will produce relief, taking care to confine your sacrification to the outside edge, so as to avoid the palatine artery and vein. Do not permit the bars to be fired.

Strangles, also a common disease of young horses, presents symptoms so like those of glanders, as to be sometimes confounded with that disease. Strangles, however, may be distinguished from glanders by the formation in the former of a continuous tumor in the hollow under the lower jaw. The treatment consists in bringing this swelling to a head, by means of a blister. As soon as it is soft on the top, it should be opened, and that by three incisions. The sore may then be dressed for a few days with emollient ointment. Cooling drinks, as cream of tartar and nitre, may be given with advantage. If there be appearance of fever, or affection of the chest, send for the surgeon, as the treatment is now beyond your skill. This, however, is rarely the case.

Poll Evil—A swelling of the poll, caused by the horse striking it against the lower edge of the manger, when raising it suddenly after stooping or by pulling upon his halter. In most cases, all attempts to prevent suppuration are useless, and I think it best to endeavor at once to hatsen it. Then open the tumor by means of a seton, which should be passed in at the top, penetrate through the bottom, and pass out at the side of the neck, just below the abscess. Foment with warm water, and keep the parts clean.

Roaring—Most generally the consequence of malformation of the larynx, but sometimes occurring as a sequel to strangles, and sometimes arising from palsy of

H. A. PALMER,

HAIRDRESSER AND PERFUMER,

DEALER IN

TOYS, JEWELRY,

Plated Ware, Tobacconists' Goods,

And Small Ware of every Description,

No. 7 SUSSEX STREET,

(Adjoining Messrs. Fingland & Draper,)

OTTAWA CITY.

the muscles connected with the larynx. The use of a strap for the cure of crib-biting is also an occasional cause. I know of no cure, and am disposed to think that, in all cases,, roaring is beyond the reach of treatment. I would also advise you not to breed from a roarer, as this defect is, in many cases, transmitted to the progeny.

Saddle-galls might have been prevented by using properly adjusted and well stuffed harness or collars. Rest the horse, bathe twice daily with warm water, and after each bathing press with spermaceti ointment.

Inflammation.—When you find a horse dull, listless, off his feed, coat staring, chest and nose hot, extremities cold, some attack of an inflammatory nature is at hand. Bleed from a large orifice until you find the pulse sensibly diminish; administer a purgative, but meanwhile let the veterinary surgeon be sent for with all speed.

Spavin.—An enlargement of the sacs of mucus placed between the tendons to prevent friction. The most common place for this to occur is at the inside of the hock, at the bend. This is called hog-spavin. When this becomes so much enlarged as to produce compression of the vein passing over it, between it and the integuments, the vein shares in the distension, and it becomes blood-spavin. In general, a spavined horse is lame, but not invariably so. Blistering, or perhaps firing, is the only cure on which I place my reliance.

Distemper generally commences in shivering, then heat of the mouth and nostrils, cough, red and heavy eye, redness of the membrane of the nose. From the commencement, there is generally, but not invariably, a discharge from the nostrils, which, in neglected cases, becomes fetid and ropy. This disease requires too much

DRUGS! DRUGS!

OTTAWA DRUG WAREHOUSE,

Dr. J. GARVEY, Proprietor.

☞ All the Novelties of the Age to be found here. ☜

HAIR DYES:

Mrs. Doctor Chevalier's Life for the Hair, Bogle's Hair Dye, Canadian Hair Dye, Batchelor's Hair Dye, Mrs. Allan's Hair Restorer and Hair Dresser, Dr. Garvey's Hair Tonic, &c., &c., &c.

ELIXIR OF CALASAYA BARK,
CIRCASSIAN HAIR RESTORER,
COCOAINE, KALISTOR,
MAGNOLIA BALM, QUININE WINE,
Italian Bitters, Old Port Wine, Cherry Wine, Brandy, (medicinal,) Stoughton Bitters, Oxygenated Bitters, Mountain Herb Bitters.

Ayer's Cherry Pectoral, Wistar's Balsam of Wild Cherry, Hall's Balsam for the Lungs, Cherry Balm, Bristol's Sarsaparilla, Ayer's Sarsaparilla, Townsend's Sarsaparilla, Swain's Aanacea, Scovill's Blood and Liver Syrup, Kennedy's Discovery and Salt Rheum Ointment.

SOLD WHOLESALE & RETAIL AT THE VERY LOWEST PRICES.

☞ TERMS CASH!!

Dr. J. GARVEY.

N. B.—Orders from Country Merchants solicited, and prompt attention given to them. Prescriptions carefully prepared.

judgment, and too much knowledge of the varied treatment called for in each different stage, for me to give you any advice further than this; if you have detected it at its very commencement, bleed copiously, and give a strong purgative,—the veterinary surgeon being also sent for. Do not suffer yourself to be made a victim of quacks. There is no specific for this disease, and under improper treatment, it is more frequently fatal than otherwise. The early attendance of a veterinary surgeon in this disease is the more desirable, as its early symptoms are extremely like those of malignant epidemic, which latter disease rapidly runs into gangrene, and terminates in death; and the former disease frequently passes into the latter, when not properly combated at first.

Broken Wind.—Incurable; but may be alleviated by condensing the food—reducing as much as possible the quantity necessary to be consumed, by giving the necessary nutriment in as small a compass as you can; as, for instance, more oats and less hay. Keep the bowels moderately open, and never work upon a full stomach. Feeding upon carrots will also be found beneficial.

Worms.—The symptoms show themselves in the appearance of the vermin in the excrements, or creeping out of the anus. Give two drachms of tartaric emetic, with twenty grains of powdered ginger every morning, fasting. When there appears much irritation about the anus give a strong dose of aloes, and inject linseed oil.

Jaundice, known by the yellowness of the eyes, mouth, and of all naked portions of the skin, with high-colored urine, dullness, and loss of appetite. Bleed: give twice daily, until the bowels have been freely opened, two drachms of aloes, with one drachm of calomel, warm white-water or thin gruel. Keep the stable cool; feed on green meats.

1867] THE RECEIPT BOOK. 105

HARAM & MONAHAN,

No. 33 RIDEAU STREET,

MANUFACTURERS AND DEALERS IN ALL KINDS OF

Upholstery and Cabinetware.

FURNITURE MADE TO ORDER AND REPAIRED,

CURTAIN CUTTING, BLIND HANGING,

OIL-CLOTH AND CARPET LAYING.

ALL KINDS OF JOBBING DONE

WITH NEATNESS AND DISPATCH.

Particular attention paid to the making of

ALL KINDS OF SHOW CASES.

Difficulty of Staling.—Give plenty of warm drink; linseed boiled in plenty of water; turpentine made into a ball with linseed meal; half an ounce of turpentine and half a drachm of ginger, with as much of the meal as is required to form the ball.

In profuse Staling (the opposite of the preceding) the treatment should be bleeding and purging; every kind of counter-irritation, astringent medicines, and feeding on carrots.

Windgalls.—An enlargement about the fetlock, caused by the enlargement of the mucus sacs, spoken of already in reference to spavin. Treatment the same.

Ringbone.— A deposit of bony matter on the cartileges and bones of the pastern and foot. The only cure is firing, and even that is only partially successful.

Thorough-pin, analagous to windgalls and spavin, being a similar enlargement above the hock, between the extensor muscle of the hock and the flexor tendons of the foot. Mode of treatment same as for windgalls.

Curb is the consequence of a strain of the tendon or its sheath, or the circular ligament which holds it in its place. It appears under the form of an enlargement at the back of the hock, two or three inches below its point. Bleed from the subcutaneous vein nearest the seat of injury; use emolient fomentations. Firing is sometimes, but not invariably, advisable. A veterinary surgeon must judge of this.

Stringhalt.—Cause and cure alike obscure. It is supposed to be an excess of nervous energy, and is usually produced by effort for heavy work. There does not appear to be any specific for the complaint.

Grease commences in inflammation of the skin of the heels, proceeding to excoriation, cracking, ulceration and fungus. Cleanse well with soap and water; use a solution of alum, or sulphate of copper, as a lotion.

[1867] THE RECEIPT BOOK. 107

THOMAS ISAAC,

(Sign of the Circular Saw)

FURNISHING IRONMONGER!

SPARKS STREET,

CENTRAL OTTAWA,

KEEPS ALWAYS IN STOCK.

IRON, CHAINS, STOVES,

GLASS, ROPES, PUTTY, &c.,

AND

General House Furnishing,

☛ AT MODERATE PRICES

Corns.—Resulting from bad shoeing, and severe work on hard roads. The effort of nature to counteract this produces a horny substance, which presses on the sensitive part of the foot, and causes lameness. Cessation from labor, and careful cutting out of the corns, with gradual work on soft ploughed land, will usually eradicate these.

Overreach.—The bruise given by an awkward blow of the toe of one foot against the heel of another. Cleanse and fasten a pledget of tow, dip't in friar's balsam upon the wound.

The preceding hints are all that would be likely to aid the amateur in the treatment of his horse. But whenever an animal worth saving displays symptoms of illness, send, without loss of time, for a professional Veterinary Surgeon.

DISEASES OF PIGS AND THEIR REMEDIES.

Points of a good Hog.—A good hog should have sufficient depth of carcass. The loin and breast should be broad. The bones should be small and the joints fine. The feet should be firm and sound. The toes be well together and press straightly on the ground. The claws also should be even, upright and healthy. The head should not have heavy bones nor be flat on the forehead. The snout should be short and curve upwards. The ear light and thin and inclined forwards.

Sows with Pigs—should have a sufficiency of wholesome, nutritious food, but not allowed to get fat. The sty should be kept clean and well littered, but not too thickly.

1867] THE RECEIPT BOOK.

Drugs! Drugs!

OTTAWA DRUG WAREHOUSE.

DR. J. GARVEY, PROPRIETOR.

All the Novelties of the Age to be found here.

Cologne, Lubin's Perfumes in every variety, Balm of a Thousand Flowers, Zozodont, Philodont, Rose Tooth Paste, (Dr. Garvey's), Rowland's Odonto, Balsam of Myrrh, Dr. Ridge's Patent Food, Feeding Bottles of every Variety—Enema's.

HORSE MEDICINES.—Gargling Oil, Black Oil, Condition Powders, Mustang Liniment, Bone and Nerve Liniment.

Trusses, Suspensary Bandages and Shoulder Braces, Sponge Bags and Bathing Caps, Essences of every kind, a large assortment of Fancy Soaps, Hair Oils too numerous to mention, and in fact every article that can be found in any Drug Store in Canada, will be kept constantly in stock at the

OTTAWA DRUG WAREHOUSE,

And sold Wholesale and Retail at the very lowest Prices.

TERMS CASH !!

Dr. J. GARVEY.

N. B.—Orders from Country Merchants solicited, and prompt attention given to them. Prescriptions carefully prepared.

Catching the Pig.—All violent measures should as far as possible be avoided. The pig is naturally averse to being handled, and in his struggles often does himself more injury than would result from the disease it is desired to remedy. One method is to catch the foot in a running noose suspended from some place, so as to draw the imprisoned foot off the ground, or envelope the head of the animal in a sack.

Administering Physic.—Whenever it is possible the medicines should be mingled with the animals food, so that it may be coaxed or cheated into taking it. When this cannot be done, let a man get the head of the animal firmly between his legs and separate the lips a little so as to form a hole, into which the fluid may be gradually poured. Should the animal snort or choke the head should be released as the animal may strangle.

Fever.—The symptoms of this disease are redness of the eyes, dryness and heat of the nostrils, the lips and the skin generally; appetite gone or very defective and generally a violent thirst. Bleed as soon as possible, after which house the animal well. The bleeding will generally be followed by a return of appetite. Do not let it eat too much. If the bowels are confined give about four ounces of equal parts castor and linseed oil.

Heavings.—This disease is really an inflammation of the lungs, and can hardly be looked on as curable. If observed in its first stage, when indicated by loss of appetite and a short dry cough, it might be got under by copious bleeding and friction, with stimulating ointment in the region of the lungs. This disease is generally caused by damp lodging, foul air and filthy food.

Catarrh.—This disease is easily cured by opening medicines followed by warm bran mash, a warm dry sty and abstinance from rich grains or stimulating diet.

THOUSANDS

CAN TESTIFY THAT

PRESTON'S
BOOT & SHOE STORE

Is the Cheapest in the City of Ottawa.

All kinds of seasonable goods, suitable to

City and Country Trade,

CONSTANTLY IN STOCK, and his style of business is

LIGHT PROFITS AND QUICK RETURNS.

Make your purchases at

NO. 12 RIDEAU STREET,

AND SAVE MONEY.

Remember, only one price is his rule. Goods purchased there that may prove unsuited to the wish of the purchaser, will be readily changed at any time, if not damaged.

Diarrhœa.—Endeavor at once to ascertain the description of food lately used by the animal as the disease may in general be traced to that. At the early stage the disease may generally be cured by change to a more binding diet. Dry lodging is indispensable and diligence requisite to keep it clean. In violent cases give some chalk in the food, or powdered egg-shells with about half a drachm of powdered rhubarb.

Crackings.—These sometimes appear on the skin of the hog particularly about the roots of the ears and tail. They should not be confounded with mange as they only result from exposure to the extremes of weather, when the animal is unable to obtain proper shelter. They are most troublesome in extreme heat if the animal have not access to water. To cure it anoint the parts with tar and lard melted together, twice or three times a day.

Foul Skin.—A simple irritation of the skin will usually yield to cleanliness and washing with a solution of chloride of lime. If neglected it may assume a malignant character, and pass rapidly into mange.

Quinsy.—This is an inflamatory affection of the glands of the throat. Shave away the hair, and rub the parts with tartar emetic ointment.

Staggers.—This is caused by a flow of blood to the head. To cure it bleed freely and purge.

Spleen.—The most positive sympton of this disease is the circumstance of the affected animal leaning towards one side, crying as it were from internal pain. Give a powerful aperient. Allow the animal to fast for four or five hours, and give some wash, in which mingle some Epsom salts. This will, in general, affect the desired end.

A. GRAHAM & CO.,

Keep constantly on hand a large and well selected stock of

FANCY AND STAPLE

DRY GOODS

READY-MADE CLOTHING,

GENTLEMEN'S UNDER GARMENTS,

Hosiery and Gloves.

Also a large assortment of Gentlemen and Youth's

HATS AND CAPS.

The above stock having been purchased during the recent fall in Goods, will be sold for CASH lower than any house in the trade.

No. 48 SPARKS STREET,

Opposite Crosby's Boot and Shoe Store.

Surfiet.—Symptoms are: panting, loss of appetite, swelling about the stomach. This will in general cure itself if all food be kept from the animal for a few hours. Then only allow it small quantities, not nearly as much as it would take. For a few days the quantity of its food should be limited, and of a liquid washy nature.

Tumors.—These are hard swellings which appear on various parts of the body. They are not formidable, and require only to be suffered to progress till they soften. Then make a free incision and press out the matter. Sulphur and nitre should be given in the food as the swellings indicate the necessity of alterative medicines.

Jaundice.—Bleed freely, diminish the quantity of food, and give dozes of aloes, combined with colocynth, every second day. The symptoms of the disease are yellowness of the white of the eye—a similar hue extending to the lips, and sometimes a swelling of the under part of the jaw.

Leprosy.—The causes of this disease are want of fresh air and foul feeding. Bleed the animal, keep him clean and give daily in his food a tablespoonful of the flour of sulphur with as much salpetre as you can take up on a sixpence.

Lethargy.—Symptoms: desire to sleep, hanging of the head, and frequently redness of the eyes. Bleed freely and give a dose of the decoction of camomile flowers or tartar emetic. Reduce the quantity of food and give a little nitre and sulphur in the morning's meal.

Murrain—Resembles Leprosy in its symptoms, with the addition of staggering, shortness of breath and discharge of viscid matter from the eyes and mouth. Keep the animal cool and clean. Bleed it and limit its food—give cloves of garlic as a purge.

JOHN P. FEATHERSTON,

𝔓harmaceutical 𝔈hemist,

—OF—

PHAR. SOC. LONDON, ENGLAND.

57, Sussex Street, Ottawa.

Measles.—Allow the animal to fast about four and twenty hours, then a warm drink, containing one drachm of carbonate of soda and one ounce of bole Armenian, wash the animal, clean the stye and change the feeding. Give at every feeding thirty grains of flower of sulphur and ten of nitre. The malady is usually brought on by dirt, or steamed food given too hot. It is troublesome to get rid of.

POULTRY AND THEIR DISEASES.

In the choice of a hen for sitting, a large bird should be selected, with large, wide-spreading wings. Though large, she must not, however, be heavy nor leggy. Elderly hens will be more willing to sit than young and giddy pullets.

Preservation of Eggs.—The best material is a mixture of mutton and beef suet, which should be melted together over a slow fire, and strain through a linen cloth into an earthen pan. The chief advantage in the use of this is, that the eggs rubbed over with it will boil as quickly as if nothing had been done to them, the fat melting off as soon as they touch the water. The transpiration is as effectually stopped by the thinnest layer of fat as by a thick coating, providing that no sensible vestige be left on the surface of the shell. All sorts of fat, grease, or oil are well adapted to this purpose; by means of butter, hog's lard, olive oil, and similar substances, eggs may be preserved for nine months as fresh as the day upon which they were laid. Eggs will also keep well when preserved in salt, by arranging them in a barrel, first a layer of salt, then a layer of eggs, alternately. This can, however, also act mechanically, like

LEATHER, HIDES, AND OIL!

GEORGE MAY,

Dealer in all kinds of

LEATHER, SHOE - FURNISHING GOODS,

SHOEMAKER'S TOOLS, TANNER'S OIL, &c.

Frank Miller's Waterproof Blacking and Harness Oil,

CASH PAID FOR HIDES.   No. 31, SUSSEX STREET.

Wholesale and Retail.

WILLIAM SUTHERLAND,

TAILOR AND CLOTHIER,
No. 61, Rideau Street.

SUITS MADE TO ORDER

FASHIONABLY, EXPEDITIOUSLY,

AND CHEAPLY.

CLOTHING, made up on the premises, always in stock.

A Fashionable Cutter, and a large number of Workmen constantly employed in the manufacture of Clothing.

bran or saw-dust, so long as the salt continues dry; for, in that case, the chlorine, which is the antiseptic principle of the salt, is not evolved. When the salt, however, becomes damp, its preservative principle will be brought into action, and may penetrate through the pores of the shell. It ought not to be overlooked, in this connection, that eggs not only spoil by the transpiration of their moisture and the putrid fermentation of their contents, in consequence of air penetrating through the pores of the shell, but also by being moved about and jostled, when carried to a distance by sea or land. Any kind of rough motion, indeed, ruptures the membranes which keep the white, the yoke, and the germ of the chicken in their appropriate places; and, upon these being mixed, putrefaction is promoted.

Rearing of Turkeys.—Much quackery has been recommended in the treatment of young turkeys. Nothing, however, should be given to them, nothing done for them; they should remain in the nest, under the shelter of their mother's wings, for at least eight or ten hours; if hatched in the afternoon, till the following morning. The hen should then be placed on the grass, in the sun, under a roomy coop. If the weather is fine, she may be stationed at any point desired, by a long piece of flannel list tied round one leg, and fastened to a stump or stone. Young turkeys are sometimes attacked by worms in the trachea; but not so often as chickens. Cramp is the most fatal to them, particularly in bad weather. A few pieces of board laid under and about the coop are useful; sometimes rubbing the leg with spirit will bring back the circulation.

Rearing of Ducklings.—None are more successful in rearing ducklings than those who keep them, for the first period of their existence, in pens two or three yards square, and cram them night and morning with

1867]   THE RECEIPT BOOK.   119

McDOUGAL & Co.,

IMPORTERS OF

GERMAN ENGLISH & AMERICAN

HARDWARE.

Sign of the Big "Augur,"

SUSSEX STREET,   OTTAWA.

R. & A. ANGUS,

Cabinet Makers and Upholsterers,

Manufacturers and importers of every style of

PLAIN AND FANCY FURNITURE,

SPRING, HAIR AND STRAW MATRESSES ALWAYS ON HAND.

FUNERAL UNDERTAKING.

WAREHOUSE—In Angus' Block, Rideau Street, Ottawa.

long, dried pellets of flour and water, or egg and flour, until they are judged old enough to be turned out with their mother to forage for themselves. They are cheerful, harmless, good-natured, cleanly creatures, carefully washing themselves, and arranging their dress, before commencing their meals; and the healthy heartiness of their appetite is amusing, rather than disgusting.

Rearing of Goslings.—For the first three or four days, goslings must be kept warm and dry, and fed on barley-meal, or oatmeal, mixed with milk, if easily procurable; if not, with water. They will begin to grow in about a week. For a week or two, they should not be turned out until late in the morning, and should always be taken in early in the evening. Their great enemy is the cramp, which can be kept off by making them sleep on dry straw. A little boiled rice, daily, assists their growth; with corn, of course, as soon as they can eat it. When goslings are first allowed to go at large with their mother, every plant of hemlock which grows within their range should be pulled up, as they are very apt to eat it, and it generally proves fatal.

Fattening.—A common method of fattening fowl is to give them the run of a farm-yard, where they thrive upon the offal of the stable and other refuse, with perhaps some small regular daily feeds; but at threshing-time, they become fat, and are styled barn-door fowls, probably the most delicate and high-flavored of all, both from their full allowance of the finest grain, and the constant health in which they are kept, by living in the natural state, and having the full enjoyment of air and exercise : or they are confined in coops during a certain number of weeks, those fowls which are soonest ready being taken as wanted. In fattening ducks, it must be remembered that their flesh will be found to partake, to a great extent, of the flavor of the food on

G. S. SUTHERLAND,
WATCH AND CLOCK MAKER,
RIDEAU STREET, OTTAWA.

Wm. McFARLANE,

MANUFACTURER OF

HEAD STONES, &c. &c.   **Chimney Pieces,** &c., &c.

Also Agent for W. & F. P. Currie's Chimney Cans, Ornamental Vases, and Sewerage Pipes.

☞ Rideau Street, next to Mathew's Hotel, Ottawa.

JOHN CULBERT,
Travelling Agent.

which they have been fattened; and as they are naturally quite indiscriminate feeders, care should be taken, for at least a week or so before killing, to confine them to select food. Boiled potatoes are very good feeding, and are still better if a little grain is mixed with them; Indian meal is both economical and nutritive, but should be used sparingly at first. Some recommend butcher's offal; but although ducks may be fattened on such food to an unusual weight, and thus be profitable for the market, their flesh will be rendered rank and gross, and not at all fit for the table.

To fatten geese, it is necessary to give them a little corn daily, with the addition of some raw Swedish turnips, carrots, mangel-wurtzel leaves, lucerne, tares, cabbage leaves, and lettuces. Barley-meal and water is recommended by some; but full-grown geese that have never been habituated to the mixture when young, will occasionally refuse to eat it. Cooked potatoes, in small quanties, do no harm; and apart from the consideration of expense, steeped wheat would produce a first-rate delicacy.

Poultry Houses.—Some people allow their fowl to roost abroad all night, in all weathers, in trees, or upon fences near the poultry-house. This is a slovenly mode of keeping even the humblest live stock; it offers a temptation to thieves, and the health of the fowls cannot be improved by their being soaked all night long in drenching rain, or having their feet frozen to the branches or rails. There is no difficulty in accustoming any sort of poultry, except the pea-fowl, to regular housing at night. It is better that turkeys should not roost in the same house with the domestic fowl, as they are apt to be cross to sitting and laying hens.

Asthma.—This common disease seems to differ sufficiently in its characteristics to warrant a distinction into

THE RECEIPT BOOK.

L. N. NYE,
TOBACCONIST,
—AND—
DEALER IN FRUIT,
WHOLESALE & RETAIL,
AND ALSO AGENT FOR THE CELEBRATED
PLANTAGENET WATER,
AT THE
SIGN of THE INDIAN CHIEF,
No. 43, Sussex Street.

THE ROYAL CANADIAN BANK.

OFFICE:

DESBARATS' UBILDINGS,

77, SPARKS STREET, OTTAWA.

INTEREST ALLOWED ON DEPOSITS.

M. P. HAYES, Agent.

two species. In one it appears to be caused by an obstruction of the air-cells, by an accumulation of phlegm, which interferes with the exercise of their functions. The fowl labors for breath, in consequence of not being able to take in the usual quantity of air at an inspiration. The capacity of the lungs is thereby diminished, the lining membrane of the windpipe becomes thickened, and its minute branches are more or less affected. These effects may, perhaps, be attributed to the fact that, as our poultry are originally natives of tropical climates, they require a more equal temperature than is afforded, except by artificial means, however well they may appear acclimated. Another variety of asthma is induced by fright, or undue excitement. It is sometimes produced by chasing fowls to catch them, by seizing them suddenly, or by their fighting with each other. In these cases, a blood-vessel is often ruptured, and sometimes one or more of the air-cells. The symptoms are: short breathing; opening of the beak often, and for quite a time; heaving and panting of the chest; and, in case of a rupture of a blood-vessel, a drop of blood appearing on the beak. Treatment: confirmed asthma is difficult to cure. For the disease in its incipient state, the fowl should be kept warm, and treated with repeated doses of hippo-powder and sulphur, mixed with butter, with the addition of a small quantity of Cayenne pepper.

Costiveness.—The existence of this disorder will become apparent by observing the unsuccessful attempts of the fowl to relieve itself. It frequently results from continued feeding on dry diet, without access to green vegetables. Indeed, without the use of these, or some substitute—such as mashed potatoes—costiveness is certain to ensue. The want of a sufficient supply of good water will also occasion the disease, on account of that

HARRIS & CAMPBELL,

CABINET MAKERS

And Upholsterers,

SUSSEX STREET, NEAR THE QUEEN'S WHARF.

Messrs. HARRIS & CAMPBELL beg to direct the attention of the public to their Cabinet Establishment, in Aumond's large stone building, near the Queen's Wharf. They are practical workmen, and guarantee to perform the best work in manufacturing or repairing all kinds of Household Furniture in the city. Tables, Chairs, Desks, Bureaus, Beds, Hair Matrasses, Spring Paliasses, and every description of Furniture made to order.

Carpets cut and laid, curtains made and put up at the lowest prices.

ONTARIO SALOON,

JOHN CAHILL, - - - - Proprietor,

Begs to announce that he has

OPENED A SALOON ON YORK STREET,

Where will be found the choicest

WINES, LIQUORS & REFRESHMENTS.

JOHN CAHILL.

peculiar structure of the fowl, which renders them unable to void their urine, except in connection with the FAECES of solid food, and through the same channel. Treatment: Soaked bread, with warm skimmed-milk, is a mild remedial agent, and will usually suffice. Boiled carrots or cabbage are more efficient. A meal of earthworms is sometimes advisable; and hot potatoes, mixed with bacon-fat, are said to be excellent. Castor-oil and burned butter will remove the most obstinate cases; though a clyster of oil, in addition, may sometimes be required, in order to effect a cure.

Diarrhœa.—The symptoms are lassitude and emaciation; and, in very severe cases, the voiding of calcareous matter, white, streaked with yellow. This resembles the yolk of a stale egg, and clings to the feathers near the vent. It becomes acrid, from the presence of ammonia, and causes inflammation, which speedily extends throughout the intestines. Treatment: This, of course, depends upon the cause. If the disease is brought on by a diet of green or soft food, the food must be changed, and water sparingly given; if it arises from undue acidity, chalk mixed with meal is advantageous, but rice-flour boluses are most reliable. Alum-water, of moderate strength, is also beneficial. In cases of bloody flux, boiled rice and milk, given warm, with a little magnesia, or chalk, may be successfully used.

Fever.—The most decided species of fever to which fowls are subject occurs at the period of hatching, when the animal heat is often so increased as to be perceptible to the touch. A state of fever may also be observed when they are about to lay. This is, generally, of small consequence, when the birds are otherwise healthy; but it is of moment, if any other disorder is present, since, in such case, the original malady will be aggravated. Fighting also frequently occasions fever, which some-

SADDLERY, HARDWARE, TRUNKS, &c.,

NO. 31, SUSSEX STREET.

large assortment of all kinds of SADDLERY, HARDWARE, Heavy, and extra Heavy HAMES, for lumbering purposes.

SOLID LEATHER TRUNKS, VALISES,

AND CARPET BAGS

Of Every Description.

GEO. MAY.

THE VARIETY HALL

No. 34 SUSSEX STREET.

General House Furnishing Establishment,

Always on hand, the best assortment in the city of

CROCKERY, CHINA & GLASSWARE,

MIRRORS AND LOOKING-GLASSES, FURNITURE OF ALL KINDS, MATRASSES, TABLE AND HALL MATS, COOKING AND BOX STOVES OF VARIOUS PATTERNS,

WHOLESALE AND RETAIL,

And at prices that defy Competition.

JOSEPH BOYDEN,
General Agent.

times proves fatal. The symptoms are an increased circulation of the blood; excessive heat; and restlessness. Treatment: Light food and change of air; and, if necessary, aperient medicine, such as castor oil, with a little burned butter.

Indigestion.—Cases of indigestion among fowls are common, and deserve attention according to the causes from which they proceed. A change of food will often produce crop-sickness, as it is called, when the fowl takes but little food, and suddenly loses flesh. Such disease is of little consequence, and shortly disappears. When it requires attention at all, all the symptoms will be removed by giving their diet in a warm state. Sometimes, however, a fit of indigestion threatens severe consequences, especially if long continued. Every effort should be made to ascertain the cause, and the remedy must be governed by the circumstances of the case. The symptoms are heaviness, moping, keeping away from the nest, the want of appetite. Treatment: Lessen the quantity of food, and oblige the fowl to exercise in an open walk. Give some powdered cayenne and gentian mixed with the usual food. Iron-rust, mixed with soft food, or diffused in water, is an excellent tonic, and is indicated when there is atrophy, or diminution of the flesh. It may be combined with oats or grain.

Lice.—The whole feathered tribe seem to be peculiarly liable to be infested with lice; and there have been instances when fowls have been so covered in this loathsome manner that the natural color of the feathers has been undistinguishable. The presence of vermin is not only annoying to poultry, but materially interferes with their growth, and prevents their fattening. They are, indeed, the greatest drawback to the success and pleasure of the poultry fanciers; and nothing but unremitting vigilance will exterminate them, and keep them exter-

1867] THE RECEIPT BOOK.

R. EATON & Co.,
Rideau Street, near the Sappers Bridge,
OTTAWA, C. W.,

LOOKING-GLASS, SILVERING
AND
MANUFACTURING WORKS!

The Subscribers are manufacturing for the Trade, and offer at very low prices, all descriptions of

HANGING, TOILET, CHIMNEY & PIER GLASSES,

They are also largely engaged in the manufacture and sale of Imitation Rosewood, Maple and Walnut Veneered Mouldings, and Washable Gilt Mouldings, Gilt Picture Frames, Ovals, &c., &c.

Also—House, Sign and Ornamental Painters, Decorators and Paper Hangers. Window Shades Painted and Lettered for stores; also, Painted & Fitted to Public Buildings and Dwellings; Curtain Fixtures and Picture Frames.

R. E. & Co undertake the Painting and Decorating of public buildings, stores and dwellings. Soiled Furniture Restained and Varnished.

Paper Hangings in endless variety of quality and pattern.

None but the best workmen are employed in the various branches of their business, and all orders with which they may be favored, will be promptly attended to at moderate prices; and they are confident of giving satisfaction in all respects.

Our Stock is extensive and complete in all departments. Inspection respectfully solicited.

PAINTS, OILS & VARNISHES
WHOLESALE & RETAIL.

R EATON, & Co.

minated. Treatment: To attain this, whitewash frequently all the parts adjacent to the roosting-pole, take the poles down and run them slowly through a fire made of wood shavings, dry weeds or other light waste combustibles. Flour of sulphur, placed in a vessel, and set on fire in a close poultry-house, will penetrate every crevice, and effectually exterminate the vermin. When a hen comes off with her brood, the old nest should be cleaned out, and a new one placed; and dry tobacco-leaves, rubbed to a powder between the hands, and mixed with the hay of the nest, will add much to the health of the poultry. Flour of sulphur may also be mixed with Indian-meal and water, and fed in the proportion of one pound of sulphur to two dozen fowls, in two parcels, two days apart. Almost any kind of grease, or unctuous matter, is also certain death to the vermin of domestic poultry. In the case of very young chickens, it should only be used in a warm, sunny day, when they should be put into a coop with their mother, the coop darkened for an hour or two, and everything made quiet, that they may secure a good rest and nap after the fatigue occasioned by greasing them. They should be handled with great care, and greased thoroughly; the hen, also. After resting, they may be permitted to come out and bask in the sun; and in a few days they will look sprightly enough. To guard against vermin, however, it should not be forgotten that cleanliness is of vital importance; and there must always be plenty of slacked lime, dry ashes, and sand, easy of access to the fowls, in which they can roll and dust themselves.

Loss of Feathers.—This disease, common to confined fowls, should not be confounded with the natural process of moulting. In this diseased state, no new feathers come to replace the old, but the fowl is left bald and naked; a sort of roughness also appears on the skin;

ALEXR. MORTIMER,

ACCOUNT BOOK MANUFACTURER,

BOOK-BINDER

AND

PAPER RULER,

No. 21, Metcalfe Street,

OPPOSITE WESLEYAN METHODIST CHURCH,

OTTAWA,

Begs to announce to his friends and patrons that he is prepared to execute all orders for

BOOK-BINDING,

PAPER-RULING, OR

BLANK-BOOK MANUFACTURING,

Of every description, in the neatest and most durable style.

Giving personal attention to all work, and having had many years practical experience, he feels confident that satisfaction will be given.

Ornamental Binding done in the most artistic style.

ALEX. MORTIMER,
Metcalfe Street.

there is a falling off in appetite, as well as moping and inactivity. Treatment : As this affection is, in all probability, constitutional rather than local, external remedies may not always prove sufficient. Stimulants, however, applied externally will serve to assist the operation of whatever medicine may be given. Sulphur may be thus applied, mixed with lard. Sulphur and cayenne, in the proportion of one quarter each, mixed with fresh butter, is good to be given internally, and will act as a powerful alterative. The diet should be changed ; and cleanliness and fresh air are indispensable. In diseased moulting, where the feathers stare and fall off, till the naked skin appears, sugar should be added to the water which the fowls drink, and corn and hemp seed be given. They should be kept warm, and occasionally be treated to doses of cayenne pepper.

Pip.—This disorder, known also as the gapes, is the most common ailment of poultry and all domestic birds. It is especially the disease of young fowls, and is most prevalent in the hottest months, being not only troublesome but frequently fatal. Treatment : Most recommend the immediate removal of the thickened membrane, which can be effected by annointing the part with butter or fresh cream. If necessary, the scab may be pricked with a needle. It will also be found beneficial to use a pill, composed of equal parts of scraped garlic and horse-raddish, with as much cayenne pepper as will outweigh a grain of wheat; to be mixed with fresh butter, and given every morning; the fowl to be kept warm. If the disease is in an advanced state, shown by the chickens's holding up its head and gaping for want of breath, the fowl should be thrown on its back, and while the neck is held straight, the bill should be opened, and a quill inserted into the windpipe, with a little turpentine. This being round, will loosen and destroy

1867] THE RECEIPT BOOK. 133

YOUNG & RADFORD,

PRACTICAL

WATCH & CLOCK MAKERS,

AND

Manufacturing Jewellers,

NO. 30 SPARKS STREET.

GOLD AND SILVER WATCHES,

GOLD AND SILVER CHAINS,

FINE GOLD JEWELRY,

ELECTRO-PLATED WARE,

AND FANCY GOODS,

ALWAYS ON HAND,

FROM THE BEST MAKERS, and of the FIRST QUALITY, WHICH WILL BE SOLD CHEAP.

———o———

All Work PERSONALLY and Promptly Attended to.

a number of small, red worms, some of which will be drawn up by the feather, and others will be coughed up by the chicken. The operation should be repeated the following day, if the gaping continues. If it ceases, the cure is effected.

Roup.—This disease is caused mainly by cold and moisture ; but it is often ascribed to improper feeding and want of cleanliness and exercise. It affects fowls of all ages, and is either acute or chronic ; sometimes commencing suddenly, on exposure ; at others gradually, as the consequence of neglected colds, or damp weather or lodging. Chronic roup has been known to extend through two years. The most prominent symptoms are difficult and noisy breathing and gaping, terminating in a rattling in the throat; the head swells, and is feverish; the eyes are swollen. and the eye-lids appear livid; the sight decays, and sometimes total blindness ensues; there are discharges from the nostrils and mouth, at first thin and limpid, afterwards thick, purulent and fetid. In this stage, which resembles the glanders in horses, the diseases becomes infectious. As secondary symptoms, it may be noticed that the appetite fails, except for drink ; the crop feels hard ; the feathers are staring, ruffled, and without the gloss that appears in health; the fowl mopes by itself and seems to suffer much pain. Treatment.—The fowls should be kept warm, and have plenty of water and scalded bran, or other light food. When chronic, change of food and air is desirable. The ordinary remedies—such as salt dissolved in water—are ineffectual. A solution of zinc, as an eye water, is valuable as cleasing application. Rue-pills, and a decoction of rue, as a tonic, have been administered with apparent benefit. The following is recommended : of powdered gentian and Jamaica Ginger, each one part; Epsom salts, one and a half parts;

HEUBACH & COWARD,

GENERAL

Commission Merchants,

FIRE, LIFE, and MARINE INSURANCE AGENTS,

AND

EXCHANGE BROKERS,

17 SPARKS STREET, OTTAWA.

DEALERS IN ALL KINDS OF COALS,

Lehigh, Blacksmith's and Newcastle Grate.

AGENTS FOR

THE MONTREAL OCEAN STEAMSHIP COMPANY.
LIVERPOOL & LONDON & GLOBE FIRE AND LIFE
    INSURANCE COMPANY.
CANADA LIFE ASSURANCE COMPANY.
COMMERCIAL UNION FIRE, LIFE AND MARINE
    ASSURANCE COMPANY.

and flour of sulphur, one part; to be made up with butter, and given every morning. Perhaps, however, the best mode of dealing with roup and all putrid affections is as follows: Take of pulverized, fresh-burnt charcoal, and of new yeast, each three parts; of pulverized sulphur, two parts; of flour, one part; of water, a sufficient quantity; mix well, and make into two doses, of the size of a a hazel-nut, and give one three times a day. Cleanliness is no less necessary than warmth; and it will sometimes be desirable to bathe the eyes and nostrils with warm milk and water, or suds, as convenient.

Wounds and Sores.—Fowls are exposed to wounds from many sources. In their frequent encounters with each other, they often result; the poultry-house is besieged by enemies at night, and, in spite of all precaution, rats, weasels, and other animals will assault the occupants of the roost, or nest, to their damage. These wounds, if neglected, often degenerate into painful and dangerous ulcers. When such injuries occur, cleanliness is the first step toward a cure. The wound should be cleared from all foreign matter, washed with tepid milk and water, and excluded as far as possible from the air. The fowl should be removed from its companions, which, in such cases, seldom or never show any sympathy, but, on the contrary, are always ready to assault the invalid, and aggravate the injury. Should the wound not readily heal, but ulcerate, it may be bathed with alum-water. The ointment of creosote is said to be effectual. Ulcers may also be kept clean, if dressed with a little lard, or washed with a weak solution of lead; if they are indolent, they may be touched with blue-stone. When severe fractures occur to the limbs of fowls, the best course, undoubtedly, to pursue—unless they are very valuable—is to kill them at once, as an act of humanity. When, however, it is deemed worth while to preserve

1867] THE RECEIPT BOOK. 137

T. KAVANAGH,

RIDEAU STREET,

FLOUR MERCHANT,

And General Grain Dealer.

---o---

The Highest Market Price Paid for Grain

OF EVERY KIND.

---o---

Always on Hand,

FLOUR, BRAN, OATMEAL,

BUCKWHEAT, &c., &c.,

All of the best quality.

them, splints may be used, when practicable. Great cleanliness must be observed; the diet should be reduced; and every precaution taken against the inflammation, which is sure to supervene. When it is established, cooling lotions—such as warm milk and water—may be applied.

MISCELLANEOUS DEPARTMENT.

Washing Fluid—Saving half the Wash-Board Labor.—Sal-soda 1 lb.; stone lime ½ lb.; water 5 qts.; boil a short time, stirring occasionally; then let it settle and pour off the clear fluid into a stone jug and cork for use; soak your white clothes over night, in simple water; wring out, and soap wrist-bands, collars, and dirty or stained places; have your boiler half filled with water, and when at scalding heat, put in one common tea-cup of the fluid, stir and put in your clothes, and boil for half an hour; then rub lightly through one suds only, rinsing well in the bluing water, as usual, and all is complete. I have found many women using turpentine, alcohol, ammonia, camphor gum, &c., in their washing fluids; but none of them ought ever to be used for such purposes (one woman lost the use of her arm, for six months, by using a fluid containing turpentine); the turpentine and alcohol especially, tend to open the pores of the skin, and thus make the person more liable to take cold in hanging out the clothes, as also to weaken the arm. And here let me say, if it is possible to avoid it, never allow the woman who washes the clothes, and thus becomes warm and sweaty, to hang them out; and especially ought this to be regarded in the winter or windy weather. Many consumptions are undoubtedly

OTTAWA BRASS FOUNDRY!

(Established 1858),

WILLIAM ST., NEXT DOOR TO THE TEA-POT,

RIDEAU STREET.

THEODORE FRIEDRICK,

Brass Founder & Finisher!

MACHINIST,

Plumber, Gas & Steam Fitter, Locksmith, Bell Hanger and Manufacturer of all kinds of work in Brass, Iron, Steel, Copper and Lead.

DEALER IN

Sheet Brass, Sheet Copper and Lead, Bar Copper, Brass and Copper wire, Brass, Iron and Copper Tubing, Lead and Gas Pipes, Gas Chandeliers and all other kinds of Gas Fixtures. Water and Beer Pumps, Patent Garden and House Engines, Locks, Keys, Coal Oil, Lamps, &c., &c.

—o—

ALSO--A SPLENDID THREE PULL BEER ENGINE.

brought on by these frequently repeated colds, in this way. It works upon the principle that two thin shoes make one cold, two colds an attack of bronchitis; two attacks of branchitis one consumption—the end, a coffin.

Liquid Blueing—For Clothes.—Most of the blueing sold is poor stuff, leaving specks in the clothes. To avoid this:—Take best Prussian-blue, pulverized, 1 oz.; oxalic acid, also pulverized, ½ oz.; soft water 1 qt. Mix. The acid dissolves the blue and holds it in evenly in the water, so that speckling will never take place. One or two table-spoons of it is sufficient for a tub of water, according to the size of the tub. Chinese-blue, when it can be got, is the best, and only costs one shilling an ounce, with three cents for the acid, will give better satisfaction than fifty cents worth of the common blueing. This amount has now lasted my family over a year.

Soft Soap.—Take white-bar soap 4 lbs; cut it fine and dissolve, by heating in soft water 4 gals.; adding sal-soda 1 lb. When all is dissolved and well mixed it is done. Yellow soap does very well, but Colgate's white, is said to be the best. But our white hard soap is the same kind. This soap can be made thicker or more thin, by using more or less water, as you may think best after once making it. Even in common soft soap, if this amount of sal-soda is put into that number of gallons, washing will be done much easier, and the soap will more than compensate for the expense and trouble of the addition.

Hard Soap, with Lard.—Sal-soda and lard, of each 6 lbs.; stone lime 3 lbs.; soft-water 4 gals.; dissolve the lime and soda in the water, by boiling, stirring, settling and pouring oil; then return to the kettle (brass or

STANISLAS ROBERT,
BUTCHER.

STALL---In his New Brick Building,

(Opposite Dr. Grant's)

RIDEAU STREET, - - OTTAWA.

Mr. ROBERT would return his sincere thanks to his numerous patrons and friends for the very generous support he has received since he commenced the Butcher business on Rideau Street, and begs to solicit a continuance of the same at his new Stall.

Customers may always rely upon procuring

THE BEST OF MEATS

from him, as he slaughters none but FIRST-CLASS animals.

MEAT DELIVERED IN ANY PART OF THE CITY
Free of Charge.

☞ ALL ORDERS PROMPTLY ATTENDED TO.

STANISLAS ROBERTS.

copper) and add the lard and boil until it becomes soap; then pour into a dish or moulds, and when cold, cut it into bars and let it dry. This recipe was obtained by finding an over-coat with it in the pocket, and also a piece of the soap; the man kept it with him, as it irritated his salt-rheum much less than other soaps. It has proved valuable for washing generally; and also for shaving purposes. It would be better than half the toilet soaps sold, if an ounce or two of sassafras oil was stirred into this amount; or a little of the soap might be put in a separate dish, putting in a little of the oil, to correspond with the quantity of soap.

White Hard Soap, with Tallow.—Fresh slacked lime, sal-soda and tallow, of each 2 lbs.; dissolve the soda in 1 gal. boiling soft water; now mix in the lime, stirring occasionally for a few hours; after which let it settle, pouring off the clear liquor and boiling the tallow therein until it is all dissolved; cool it in a flat box or pan, and cut into bars or cakes, as preferred. It can be flavored with sassafras oil, as the last, by stirring it in when cool; it can be colored also, if desired, as mentioned in the "Variegated Toilet Soap." When any form of soda is used in making soap, it is necessary to use lime to give it causticity; or in other words, to make it caustic; which gives it much greater power upon the grease, by removing the carbonic acid; hence the benefit of putting lime in the bottom of a leach when making soap from common ashes.

Transparent Soap.—Take nice yellow bar soap, 6 lbs.; cut it thin and put into a brass, tin, or copper kettle; with alcohol $\frac{1}{2}$ gal.; heating gradually over a slow fire, stirring until all is dissolved; then add an ounce of sassafras essence, and stir until well mixed; now pour into pans about $1\frac{1}{2}$ inches deep, and when cold cut into square bars, the length or width of the pan as desired.

DR. JOHN LEGGO,

Surgeon Dentist,

HUNTON'S BLOCK,

SPARKS STREET, CENTRAL OTTAWA.

TEETH EXTRACTED WITHOUT PAIN, by means of ETHEREAL SPRAY.

Dr. C. LEGGO,

Physician, Surgeon, and Accoucheur,

Office—HUNTON'S BLOCK, SPARKS STREET,

CENTRAL OTTAWA.

This gives you a nice toilet soap for a trifling expense, and when fully dry it is very transparent.

One Hundred Pounds of Good Soap for $1.30.—Take potash 6 lbs., 75 cts.; lard 4 lbs., 50 cts.; resin ¼ lb., 5 cts. Beat up the resin, mix all together, and set aside for five days; then put the whole ten gallon cask of warm water, and stir twice a day for ten days; at the expiration of which time you will have one hundred pounds of excellent soap.

Windsor, or Toilet Soap.—Cut some new, white bar soap into thin slices, melt it over a slow fire, and scent it with oil of caraway; when perfectly dissolved, pour it into a mould and let it remain a week, then cut it into such sized squares as you may require it.

Tallow Candles for Summer Use.—Most tallow in summer, is more or less soft, and often quite yellow. To avoid both: Take your tallow and put a little bees-wax with it, especially if your bees-wax is dark and not fit to sell; put into a suitable kettle, adding weak ley and gently boil, an hour or two each day for two days, stirring and skimming well; each morning cutting it out and scrapping off the bottom which, is soft, adding fresh ley (be sure it is not too strong) 1 or 2, or 3 gals., according to the amount of tallow. The third morning use water in which alum and saltpetre are dissolved, at the rate of 1 pound each, for 30 lbs. of tallow; then simmer, stir, and skim again; let cool, and you can take it off the water for use. They may be dipped or run in moulds; for dipping, allow two pounds for each dozen candles. Salpetre and alum are said to harden lard for candles: but it is amongst the humbugs of the day. But I will give you a plan which is a litter shorter for hardening tallow; either will work well, take your choice:

2 Tallow—To Cleanse and Bleach.—Dissolve alum 5

1867] THE RECEIPT BOOK.

JOHN ROOS,
Wholesale & Retail
TOBACCONIST!

SPARKS STREET,

HAS THE FINEST ASSORTMENT OF

SMOKING AND CHEWING TOBACCOS,

IN THE CITY; ALSO,

PIPES AND CIGAR HOLDERS!

Of every Pattern and Material.

POUCHES & TOBACCO BOXES

IN GREAT VARIETY.

Cigars & Snuffs of the Choicest Brands,

Every article of good quality and reasonable in price. Country dealers supplied at most advantageous rates.

lbs. in water 10 gals., by boiling; and when it is dissolved add tallow 20 lbs.; continue the boiling for an hour, constanty stirring and skimming; when sufficiently cool to allow it, strain through thick muslin; then set aside to harden; when taken from the water, lay it by for a short time to drip. Dip or mould, as you please, not expecting them to "run" in summer nor "crack" in winter. They will also burn very brilliantly, at which, however, you will not be surprised when you consider the amoun of filth thrown off in cleansing.

Beef—To Pickle for Long Keeping.—First, thoroughly rub salt into it and let it remain in bulk for twenty-four hours to draw off the blood. Second, take it up let it drain, and pack as desired. Third, have ready a pickle prepared as follows: For every 100 lbs. of beef used, 7 lbs of salt; saltpetre and cayenne pepper, of each 1 oz.; molasses 1 quart, and soft water 8 gals.; boil and skim well, and when cold pour it over the beef. This amount will cover one hundred pounds, if it has been properly packed. I have found persons who use nothing but salt with the water, and putting on hot again The only object claimed for putting the brine on the meat while hot, is, that it hardens the surface, which retains the juices instead of drawing them of.

The Michigan Farmer's method—Is, "for each 100 lbs of beef, use salt 5 lbs; saltpetre $\frac{1}{4}$ oz; brown sugar, 1 lb; dissolve in sufficient water to cover the meat—two weeks after take up, drain—throw away the brine, make more the same as first; it will keep the season through. When to be boiled for eating, put into boiling water—for soups, into cold water." I claim a preference for the first plan, of drawing off the blood before pickling, as saving layer; and that the cayenne and saltpetre improves the flavor and helps to preserve; and that boiling and skimming cleanse the brine very much.

1867] THE RECEIPT BOOK.

HENEY & CO.,

(SIGN OF THE WHITE HORSE,)

English Saddles, Bridles, and Martingales, Silver-plated and Japanned Double and Single Harness, made of English Oak-tanned Leather; English, American, and Canadian Whips,

Brushes, Curry-combs, Sponges, Harris' Harness Composition; a large stock of

COARSE HARNESS,

suited for Lumberers and Farmers, always on hand; Imported Horse Clothing, in Suits or Sheets, very superior.

Also a large assortment of

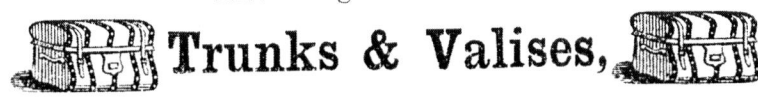

Trunks & Valises,

Consisting of Ladies' and Gents' Saratogas; French Solid Leather Jenny Linds, &c., &c.

Every Article in the Trade Constantly on Hand.

☞ Ordered work and repairing promptly attended to.

No. 24 York Street,

SIGN OF THE WHITE HORSE.

Mutton Hams.—to Pickle for Drying.—First take weak brine and put the hams into it for 2 days, then pour off and apply the following, and let it remain on from two to three weeks, according to size: For each 100 lbs., take salt 6 lbs.; saltpetre, 1 oz; salaratus, 2 oz; molasses, 1 pt.; water, 6 gals., will cover these if closely packed. The salaratus keeps the mutton from becoming too hard.

Pork—to have fresh from Winter Killing, for Summer Frying.—Take pork when killed in the early part of the winter, and let it lie in pickle about a week or ten days; or until sufficiently salted to be palatable; then slice it up and fry it about half or two-thirds as much as you would for present eating; now lay it by in its own grease, in jars properly covered, in a cool place, as you would lard. When desired, in spring or summer, to have fresh pork, take out what you wish and re-fry suitable for eating, and you have it as nice as can be imagined. Try a jar of it, and know that some things can be done as well as others. It is equally applicable to hams and shoulders, and I have no doubt it will work as well upon beef, using lard sufficient to cover it. So well satisfied am I of it that I have put in beef-steak this spring, with my fresh ham, in frying for summer use. It works upon the principle of canning fruits to exclude the air. I put in no bone.

Peaches and Pears.—After paring and coring, put amongst them sufficient sugar to make them palatable for present eating,—about 3 to 4 lbs. only for each bushel; let them stand a while to dissolve the sugar, not using any water; then heat to a boil, and continue the boiling, with care, from 20 to 30 minutes; or sufficiently long to heat through, which expels the air. Have ready a kettle of hot water, into which dip the can long enough to heat it; then fill in the fruit while hot, cork.

THE RECEIPT BOOK.

THE SUBSCRIBER BEGS LEAVE TO INTIMATE THAT HE HAS JUST OPENED A FIRST-CLASS

FAMILY GROCERY,

IN WILLS' BRICK BUILDING,

No. 52 SUSSEX STREET,

Where he is prepared to furnish his friends and the public with every article usually kept in a First-class Grocery Establishment.

———o———

HIS STOCK OF

TEAS, COFFEES, SUGARS, SPICES,

SOAPS, AND GENERAL GROCERY GOODS,

Are all new, and of the First Quality, and have been selected by himself in the best markets. They will be found superior in quality and low in price. His stock of

LIQUORS, GLASSWARE & CROCKERY,

is full and complete, and equal in all respects to that of any house in the trade.

☞ A call is respectfully solicited.

JOHN LYONS.

ing it immediately, and dip the end of the cork into the "Cement for Canning Fruits." When cold it is best to dip the second time to make sure that no air holes are left which would spoil the fruit. All canned fruits are to be kept in a very cool cellar. We have, yesterday and to-day, been eating peaches put up in this way, two years ago, which were very nice indeed.

Berries, Plums, Cherries, &c.—Raspberries, blackberries, whortleberries, currents, cherries and plums, need not be boiled over ten to fifteen minutes; using sugar to make palatable, in all cases; as it must be put in some time, and it helps to preserve the fruit. They require the same care in heating cans, &c., as above for peaches.

Strawberries.—For strawberries, put sugar $\frac{1}{2}$ lb. for each lb. of berries; and proceed as for berries above. Strawberries are so juicy, and have such a tendency to fermentation, that it is almost impossible to keep them. I have found it absolutely so, until I adopted the plan of using the amount of sugar above named: if others can do with less, they can benefit the public by telling me how they do it.

Tomatoes.—For tomatoes, scald and peel them as for other cooking; then scald, or rather boil for about 15 minutes only, and can as above. Or what I think best, is to use a little salt, and put them into half-gallon jugs; for we want them in too great quantities to stop on a few glass jars, such as we use for other fruit; as for tin cans, I never use them; if you do use tin cans for tomatoes it will not do to use salt with them, as it has a tendency to cause rust.

Cement for Canning Fruits.—eRsin 1 lb.; lard, tallow and beeswax, of each 1 oz. Melt and stir together; and have it hot, ready to dip into when canning.

[1867]   THE RECEIPT BOOK.

SATCHELL BROS.,

No. 7, NEW MARKET,

OTTAWA,

Butchers to His Excellency Lord Monck,

KEEP CONSTANTLY ON HAND,

SUPERIOR STALL FED BEEF,

CORNED BEEF, SPICED BEEF, and PICKLED TONGUE.

Steamboats, Hotels, & Families

Supplied with the

VERY BEST OF MEATS

On the shortest notice and most reasonable terms.

All orders received will be delivered to any part of the city

FREE OF CHARGE.

Tomato Preserves.—As some persons will have preserves, I give them the plan of making the most healthy of any in use: The ripe, scalded and peeled tomatoes, 13 lbs.; nice, scalding hot molasses 1 gal.; pour the molasses upon them and let stand 12 hours; then boil until they are properly cooked; now skim out the tomatoes, but continue boiling the syrup until quite thick; then pour again upon the tomatoes, and put away as other preserves. A table-spoon of ginger tied up in a bit of cloth, and boiled in them, gives a nice flavor; or the extracts can be used; or lemon peel, as preferred —if sugar is used, pound for pound is the amount. But I prefer to put them, or any other fruit, into jugs, cans, or bottles, which retains the natural flavor and does not injure the stomach, which all preserves do, to a greater or less extent. Yet I give you another, because it does so nicely in place of citron, in cakes.

Preserved Water-Melon in place of Citron, for Cakes. —The harder part of water-melon; next the skin, made into preserves, with sugar, equal weights; cooking down the syrup rather more for common use, causes it to granulate, like citron, which is kept for sale. This chopped fine, as citron, makes an excellent substitute for that article; and for much less cost. Call in the neighbours, to help eat about a dozen good sized melons, and you have outside enough for the experiment; and if the doctor is near he will help without a fee. They are nice, also, in mince pies in place of raisins.

Currants—to Dry with Sugar.—Take fully ripe currants, stemmed, 5 lbs.; sugar, 1 lb.; put into a brass kettle, stirring at first, then as the currants boil up to the top, skip them off; boil down the juicy syrup until quite thick, and pour it over the currants, mixing well, then place on suitable dishes, and dry them by placing in a low box, over which you can place musketo-bar, to keep

1867] THE RECEIPT BOOK. 153

H. F. MacCARTHY,

APOTHECARY.

—o—

MEDICAL HALL,

Wellington Street.

—o—

IMPORTER

—o—

WHOLESALE & RETAIL!

—o—

Storekeepers Supplied at Moderate Prices.

PRESCRIPTIONS PROMPTLY ATTENDED TO.

away flies. When properly dried, put in jars and tie paper over them. Put cold water upon them and stew as other fruit for eating or pie-making, adding more sugar if desired.

Tinware—to Mend by the Heat of a Candle.—Take a vial about two-thirds full of muriatic acid, and put into it little bits of sheet zinc, as long as it dissolves them; then put in a crumb of sal-ammoniac, and fill up with water, and it is ready to use. With the cork of the vial wet the place to be mended, with the preparation; then put a piece of sheet zinc ove the hole and hold a lighted candle or spirit lamp under the place, which melts the solder on the tin and causes the zince to adhere without further trouble. Wet the zinc also with the solution. Or a little solder may be put on in place of the zinc, or with the zinc.

Water Filter—Home Made.—Rain water is much healthier than hard water as a beverage; and the following will be found an easy and cheap way to fit for drinking purposes: Have an oak tub made, holding from half, to a barrel, according to the amount of water needed in the family; let it stand on end, with a faucet near the bottom; or, I prefer a hole through the bottom, near the front side, with a tube in it which prevents the water from rotting the outside of the tub; then put clean pebbles 3 or 4 incfles in thickness over the bottom of the tub; now have charcoal pulverized to the size of small peas (that made from hard maple is best) and put in a half bushel or so at a time; pound it down quite firmly, then put in more and pound again until the tub is filled to within 8 inches of the top; and again put on 2 inches more of pebbles; then put a piece of clean white flannel over the whole top as a strainer. The flannel can be washed occasionally, to remove the impurities collected from the water, and it might be well to put a flannel be-

THE RECEIPT BOOK.

D. R. LEAVENS,

WHOLESALE AND RETAIL DEALER IN

ROCK

AND

KEROSINE OIL,

Lamps, Chimneys, Wicks, Burning Fluid,

MACHINE OIL, BENZOLE,

73 Sussex Street, Ottawa.

SIGN,—RED BARREL.

AGENT FOR THE WANZER SEWING MACHINE.

tween the pebbles and flannel at the bottom also. When the charcoal becomes foul, it can be renewed as before, but will work a whole season without renewing. Put on your water freely until it becomes clear; when you will be as wel satisfied, as you would be if it ran through a patent filter, costing six times as much as this. A large jar to hold the filtered water can be set in an ice-box if preferred; or an occasional piece of ice can be put in the water; but if the filter is set in the cellar, as it should be, the water will be sufficiently cool for er you get the Russian, for thirty seven cents per ounce. is as low as the genuine article can be purchased in small quantities, whilst the common bears a price of only from ten to 12 cents, and even less.

Weeds.—The following method to destroy weeds is pursued at the mint in Paris, with good effect: Water 10 gal.; stone lime 20 lbs.; flour of sulphur 2 lbs. Boil in an iron kettle; after settling, the clear part is to be poured off and sprinkled freely upon the weedy walks. Care must be taken, for it will destroy weeds; and as certainly destroy edging and border flowers, if sprinkled on them.

Cement for China, &c., which stands Fire and Water. —With a small camel's hair brush, rub the broken edges with a little carriage oil varnish. If neatly put together, the fracture will hardly be perceptible, and when thoroughly dry will stand both fire and water.

Russian Cement.—Much is said about cements; but there is probably nothing so white and clear, and certainly not better than the following: Russian ising-glass dissolved in pure soft water, snow water is best; for it takes twelve hours to soften it by soaking in pure soft water, then considerable heat to dissolve it; after which it is applicable to statuary, china, glass, alabaster, &c., &c. In all cements the pieces must be secured until

[1867]   THE RECEIPT BOOK.   157

JOHN DURIE & SON,
IMPORTERS,
General Booksellers and Stationers,
WHOLESALE AND RETAIL.

Miscellaneous, School & Juvenile Books,
SCHOOL, OFFICE, AND COUNTING HOUSE STATIONERY.

Family, Pew and Pocket Bibles,
Prayer Books, Church Services and Hymn Books,
All New Books kept in Stock, or procured to order.

T. RAJOTTE,

Begs leave to announce to the inhabitants of Ottawa and the surrounding country the fact that he has commenced business as manufacturer of

CLOTHING OF EVERY DESCRIPTION,

Importer of Cloths, Tweeds, &c.,

WHOLESALE AND RETAIL,

No. 32 SPARKS STREET, OTTAWA.

dry. It is easy to reason that if twelve to fifteen hours are required to soften this isinglass that no dish-washing will ever effect it. You may judge from the price whethhealth. This makes a good cider filter, also, first straining the cider through cotton to free it from the coarest pomace.

Cement, Cheap and Valuable.—A durable cement is made by burning oyster shells, and pulverizing the lime from them very fine ; then mixing it with white of egg to a thick paste, and applying it to the china or glass, and securing the pieces together until dry. When it is dry, it takes a very long soaking for it to become soft again. I have lifted thirty pounds by the stem of a wine-glass which had been broken, and mended with this cement. Common lime will do, but it is not so good; either should be fresh burned, and only mix what is needed, for whence once dry you cannot soften it.

Cement—Water-proof, for Cloth or Belting.—Take ale 1 pt. ; best Russia isinglass 2 oz. ; put them into a common glue kettle and boil until the isinglass is dissolved, then add 4 oz. of the best common glue, and dissolve it with the other ; then slowly add $1\frac{1}{2}$ ozs. of boiled linseed oil, stirring all the time when adding, and until well mixed. When cold it will resemble India-rubber. When you wish to use this, dissolve what you need in a suitable quantity of ale to have the consistence of thick glue. It is applicable for earthenware, china, glass, or leather, for harness bands for machinery, cloth belts for cracker machines for bakers, &c., &c. If for leather, shave off as if for sewing, apply the cement with a brush while hot, laying a weight to keep each joint firmly for 6 to 10 hours, or over night. This cement will supersede Spaulding's Prepared Glue, and all the white cements you can scare up, if you use good articles to make it of—not less than thirty or forty cents a pound for common glue,

P. GELHAUSEN,
TOBACCONIST,
No. 21 RIDEAU STREET,

Has always on hand the choicest brands of

TOBACCOS, CIGARS & SNUFF

At reasonable prices. Also, an extensive assortment of

MEERSCHAUM, BRIAR-ROOT AND CLAY PIPES,

POUCHES, CIGAR HOLDERS, &c., &c.

GEORGE COX,

Card and Seal Engraver,

AND

PLAIN & COLORED EMBOSS PRINTER,

SPARKS STREET,

(Near the Russell House),

OTTAWA.

and three shillings per ounce for the Russian isinglass; but the expense of this will cause it only to be used when dampness is to be contended with. If you have not a glue kettle, take an oyster can and punch some holes through the top of it, putting in a string to suspend it on a stick in a common kettle of boiling water, and keep it boiling in that way.

Cement, or Furniture Glue, for House Use.—To mend marble, wood, glass, china, and ornamental ware—take water 1 gallon; nice glue 3 lbs.; white lead 4 ozs.; whiskey 3 qts.; mix by dissolving the glue in the water; remove from the fire and stir in the white lead, then add the whisky, which keeps it fluid, except in the coldest whether. Warm and stir it up when applied.

White Cement.—Take white (fish) glue, 1 lb. 10 oz.; dry white lead 6 ozs.; soft water 3 pts.; alcohol 1 pt. Dissolve the glue by putting into a tin kettle, or dish, containing the water, and set this dish into a kettle of water, to prevent the glue from being burned; when the glue is all dissolved, put in the lead and stir and boil until all is thorougly mixed; remove from the fire, and when cool enough to bottle, add the alcohol, and bottle while it is yet warm, keeping it corked. This last recipe has been sold about the country for from twenty-five cents to five dollars, and one man gave a horse for it.

German Cement.—Two measures of litharge, and 1 each of unslaked lime and flint glass; each to be pulverized separately before mixing; then to use it, wet it up with old drying-oil. The Germans use it for glass and china ware only. Water hardens it instead of softening.

Scrap-Book Paste, or Cement.—A piece of common glue 2 square inches; dissolve it in water, adding as

1867] THE RECEIPT BOOK. 161

Apothecaries' Hall,
WELLINGTON STREET OTTAWA.

JOSEPH SKINNER,

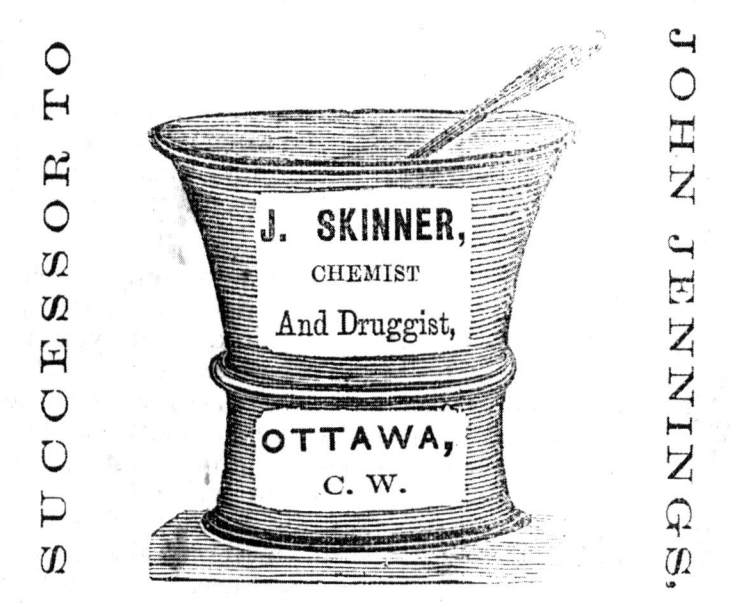

SUCCESSOR TO

J. SKINNER,
CHEMIST
And Druggist,

OTTAWA,
C. W.

JOHN JENNINGS,

Wholesale and Retail
CHEMIST & DRUGGIST,
AND DEALER IN

Paints, Oils, Varnishes, Dye-Stuffs, Seeds, Patent Medicines, &c., &c.

BEST COAL OIL AT LOWEST PRICES.

much pulverized alum in weight, as of the glue; now mix flour ½ teaspoonful in a little water; stir it in and boil. When nearly cool stir in oil of lavender 2 teaspoons. This should make a pint of paste, which will keep a long time if tightly covered when not in use.

Preventing Leaks about Chimneys, &c.—Dry sand 1 pt.; ashes 2 pts.; clay dried and pulverized 3 pts.; all to be pulverized and mixed into a paste with linseed oil. Apply it while soft, as desired, and when it becomes hard water will have no effect on it. It may be used for walks and I think it would do well in cisterns, and on roofs, &c.

Rat Exterminator.—Flour 3 lbs.; water only sufficient to make it into a thick paste; then dissolve phosphorus 1 oz., in butter 1½ ozs., by heat. Mix. This you will leave, thickly spread on bread, where rats can get at it; or make into balls, which is preferable, covered or rolled with sugar. If it is desired to settle this article and you wish to color or hide its composition, work into it pulverized turmeric 2 ozs. Take warm water 1 qt.; lard 2 lbs.; phosphorus 1 oz. Mix and thicken with flour. It is found best to make only in small quantities, as the phosphorus looses its power by exposure. Some will object to killing rats about the house; but I had rather smell their dead carcases than taste their tail prints, left on everything possible for them to get at, or suffer loss from their tooth prints on all things possible for them to devour or destroy.

Death for the Old Sly Rat.—Some rats get so cunning that it is almost impossible to overcome their shrewdness. Then get a few grains of strychnine, having a little fresh lean meat broiled; cut it into small bits, by using a fork to hold it, for if held by the fingers, they will smell them and not heat it; cutting with a sharp

1867] THE RECEIPT BOOK.

Competition Defied!

H. & J. GOWAN

Wish to inform the citizens of Ottawa and vicinity that they have

Removed to Centre Town,

NEARLY OPPOSITE TO BISHOP'S HOTEL,

Where they intend to manufacture all descriptions of Portrait, Picture, Photograph and Looking-glass

FRAMES,

Window Cornices and other Ornamental Brackets, &c., &c., on Shortest Notice.

AND WILL ALSO

Clean All Kinds of Gilding,

AND RE-GILD IF REQUIRED.

☞ Oil Paintings Cleaned, and all Marks and Stains taken out of Engravings, making them look like new. Maps Mounted and Varnished, and all kinds of Cornices Cleaned and Lacquered.

N. B.—Engravings bought and taken in exchange.

J. H. GOWAN

Is prepared to furnish, at the shortest notice, BRASS and STRING BANDS, with any required number of instruments, for Balls, Parties, and Pic-nics.

pen-knife; then cut a little hole into the bits, and put in a little of the strychnine, and close up the meat together. Put these on a plate where they frequent, but not near their holes, laying a piece of paper over the meat; when these are eaten put more, for three or four days, and you are soon done with the wisest of them.

To Drive Away Alive.—If you choose to drive them away alive, take potash pulverized, and put quite plenty of it into all their holes about the house. If the potash is pulverized and left in the air, it becomes pasty; then it can be daubed on the boards or planks, where they come through into rooms. They will sooner leave, than be obliged to have a continual re-application of this "Doctor Stuff," every time they go through their holes.

Straw and Chip Hats—To Varnish Black.—Best alcohol 4 ozs.; pulverized, black sealing-wax 1 oz.; put them into a vial, and put the vial into a warm place, stirring or shaking occasionally, until the wax is dissolved; apply it when warm, by means of a soft brush, before the fire or in the sun. It gives stiffness to old straw hats or bonnets, makes a beautiful gloss, and resists wet; if anything else is required, just apply it to small baskets only, and see how nicely they will look.

Straw Bonnets—To Color a Beautiful Slate.—First soak the bonnet in rather strong warm suds for fifteen minutes, this is to remove sizing or stiffening; then rinse in warm water, to get out the soap; now scald cudbear 1 oz., in sufficient water to cover the hat or bonnet—work the bonnet in this dye at 180 degrees of heat, until you get a little purple; now have a bucket of cold water blued with the extract of indigo, about $\frac{1}{2}$ oz., and work or stir the bonnet in this, until the tint pleases. Dry, then rinse out with cold water and dry again, in the shade. If you get the purple too deep in shade, the final slate will be too dark.

1867] THE RECEIPT BOOK. 165

ROBERTSON, LAWRENCE & CO.,

TAILORS & GENERAL OUTFITTERS,

SPARKS STREET,

OPPOSITE THE RUSSELL HOUSE,

CENTRAL OTTAWA.

Whitewashes and Cheap Paints.—Brilliant Stucco Whitewash—Will last on Brick or Stone, twenty to thirty years.—Many have heard of the brilliant stucco whitewash on the east end of the President's house at Washington. The following is a recipe for it, as gleaned from the "National Intelligencer, with some additional improvements learned by experiments : Nice unslacked lime ½ bushel ; slack it with boiling water ; cover it during the process, to keep in the steam. Strain the liquid through a fine sieve or strainer, and add to it, salt 1 peck ; previously well dissolved in water ; rice 3 lbs. —boiled to a thin paste, and stirred in boiling hot; Spanish whiting ½ lb. ; clean nice glue 1 lb., which has been previously dissolved by sooking it well, and then hanging it over a slow fire, in a small kettle, immersed in a larger one filled with water. Now add hot water 5 gals., to the mixture, stir it well, and let it stand a few days covered from the dirt. It should be put on hot. For this purpose it can be kept in a kettle on a portable furnace. Brushes more or less small may be used, according to neatness of job required. It answers as well as oil paint for brick or stone, and is much cheaper. Coloring matter, dissolved in whiskey, may be put in and made of any shade you like ; Spanish brown stirred in will make red-pink, more or less deep, according to quantity. A delicate tinge of this is very pretty for inside walls.

Whitewash—Very Nice for Rooms.—Take whiting 4 lbs. ; white or common glue 2 ozs. ; stand the glue in cold water over night ; mix the whiting with cold water, and heat the glue until dissolved ; and pour it into the other hot. Make of a proper consistence to apply with a common whitewash brush. Use these proportions for a greater or less amount. In England scarcely any other kind of whitewash is used.

LIVERY STABLES,

CORNER METCALFE and ALBERT STREETS,

P. BUCKLEY - PROPRIETOR.

CONSTANTLY FOR HIRE,

Vehicles Suited to every Kind of Travel,

ALSO, A NUMBER OF WELL-TRAINED

CARRIAGE HORSES,

And SADDLE-HORSES for Ladies and Gentlemen.

Parties leaving orders at the stables may depend on having their wishes

Promptly and Attentively Carried Out.

---o---

This establishment has for a number of years enjoyed the patronage of the leading families of Toronto, Ottawa, and Quebec, and in all cases

Perfect Satisfaction

has been expressed at the style of the animals and vehi l furnished, and at the MODERATE RATES CHARGED

Paint—To make without Lead or Oil.—Whiting 5 lbs.; skimmed milk 2 qts.; fresh slaked lime 2 ozs. Put the lime into a stoneware vessel, pour upon it a sufficient quantity of the milk to make a mixture resembling cream; the balance of the milk is then to be added; and, lastly, the whiting is to be crumbled upon the surface of the fluid, in which it gradually sinks. At this period it must be well stirred in, or ground as you would other paint, and it is fit for use. There may be added any coloring matter that suits the fancy, (see the first whitewash for mixing colors,) to be applied in the same manner as other paints, and in a few hours it will become perfectly dry. Another coat may then be added and so on until the work is done.

Black and Green Paint—Durable and Cheap, for Out-Door Work.—Any quantity of charcoal, powdered; a sufficient quantity of litharage as a dryer, to be well levigated (rubbed smooth) with linseed oil; and, when used, to be thinned with well boiled linseed oil. The above forms a good black paint. By adding yellow ochre, an excellent green is produced, which is preferable to the bright green, used by painters, for all garden work, as it does not fade with the sun.

Milk Paint, for Barns—Any Color.—" Mix water lime with skim-milk, to a proper consistence to apply with a brush, and it is ready to use. It will adhere well to wood, whether smooth or rough, to brick, mortar or stone, where oil has not been used, (in which case it cleaves to some extent) and forms a very hard substance, as durable as the best oil paint. It is too cheap to estimate, and any one can put it on who can use a brush. Any color may be given to it, by using colors of the tinge desired, dissolving in whiskey first, then adding in to suit the fancy, as in the first recipe. If a red is pre-

GEORGE HAY,
IMPORTER,
AND WHOLESALE AND RETAIL DEALER IN

Shelf and Heavy Hardware,

SPARKS STREET,
OTTAWA.

ROGERS' CELEBRATED CUTLERY,
Table and Pocket.

GUNS, POWDER, SHOT, &c.; FISHING TACKLE, &c.; BRITANNIA AND PLATED WARE; HOUSE FURNISHINGS, VERY COMPLETE.

Stones of Every Description,

PAINTS, GLASS, PUTTY, &c.; BRUSHES—ALL KINDS; OILS, LAMPS and MACHINERY.

FIRE-PROOF SAFES,

Scales — Warehouse, Counter, &c.; Mechanics' Tools, Builders' Hardware, Iron, Steel; Smiths' Coals;

AGRICULTURAL IMPLEMENTS
of all kinds in Stock, or ordered.

ferred, mix Venetian-red with milk, not using any lime. It looks well for fifteen years.

Liquid and Water-Proof Glues—Liquid Glue.—To have a good glue always ready for use, just put a bottle two thirds full of best common glue, and fill up the bottle with common whisky; cork it up, and set by 3 or 4 days, and it will dissolve without the application of heat. It will keep for years, and is always ready to use without heat, except in very cold weather, when it may need to be set a little while in a warm place, before using.

Imitation of Spalding's Glue.—First, soak in cold water, all the glue you wish to make at one time, using only glass. earthern, or porcelain dishes; then by gentle heat dissolve the glue in the same water, and pour in a little nitric acid, sufficient to give the glue a sour taste, like vinegar, or from ½ oz. to 1 oz., to each pound of glue. The acid keeps it in a liquid state, and prevents it from spoiling; as nice as Spalding's or any other, for a very trifling expense. If iron dishes are used, the acid corrodes them and turns the glue black. Or Acetic acid 1 oz.; pure soft water 6 oz.; glue 3 oz.; gum tragacanth 1 oz. Mix, and if not as thick as desired, add a little more glue. This keeps in a liquid state, does not decompose; and is valuable for druggists in labeling; also for house use; and if furniture men were not prejudiced, they would find it valuable in the shop.

Water-Proof Glue—Is made by first soaking the glue in cold water, for an hour or two, or until it becomes a little soft, yet retaining its original form; then taking it from the water, and dissolving it by gentle heat, stirring in a little boiled linseed-oil. If mahogany vaneers were put on with this glue, they would not fall off, as they now do, by the action of the atmosphere.

THE UNION HOUSE,

GEORGE ARMSTRONG - PROPRIETOR,

Corner Queen and Elgin Streets.

OTTAWA.

EVERY CONVENIENCE AND COMFORT FOR THE TRAVELLING PUBLIC.

---o---

The Bar always supplied with the

CHOICEST LIQUORS,

AND THE TABLE SPREAD WITH

EVERY DELICACY OF THE SEASON.

---o---

Good Stabling and an Attentive Hostler.

Fire Kindlers.—To make very nice fire kindlers, take rosin, any quantity, and melt it, putting it for each lb. being used, from 2 to 3 ozs. of tallow, and when all is hot, stir in pine sawdust to make very thick; and, while yet hot, spread it out about 1 inch thick upon boards which have fine saw-dust sprinkled upon them, to prevent it from sticking. When cold break up into lumps about 1 inch square. But if for sale take a thin board and press upon it, while yet warm, to lay it off into one inch squares; this makes it break regularly, if you press the crease sufficiently deep, greasing the marking-board to prevent it from sticking. One of these blocks will easily ignite with a match, and burn with a strong blaze long enough to kindle any wood fit to burn. The above sells readily in all our large towns and cities, at a great profit.

Starch Polish.—White-wax 1 oz.; spermaceti 2 ozs.; melt them together with a gentle heat. When you have prepared a sufficient amount of starch, in the usual way, for a dozen pieces—put into it a piece of the polish the size of a large pea; more or less, according to large or small washings. Or, thick gum solution (made by pouring boiling water upon gum arabic), one table-spoon to a pint of starch, gives clothes a beautiful gloss.

PAYNE'S BEE-KEEPING FOR THE MANY.

Bee-houses of all kinds I very much dislike; many hives are ruined by them; they are expensive in the first place, and they form a shelter for their worst enemies, mice, moths, spiders, &c., and not the least, dampness, which is ruinous to them. I would recommend

TEMPLE OF FASHIONS.

P. A. EGLESON,

MERCHANT TAILOR

No. 50 SUSSEX STREET,

OTTAWA CITY.

the hives being placed south, or as nearly so as may be convenient; if at all varying from it, give them a little inclination to the east, and be sure to place them so that they have the morning sun, for the honey-gathering for the day usually finishes by two o'clock; therefore an hour in the morning is of much importance to the bees, as well as to their proprietors. Another inconvenience arising from bee-houses is, that several hives being placed upon the same board encourages pilfering, and renders it almost impossible to operate upon one hive without disturbing the whole.

Stand for Hive.—Having, therefore, for these reasons, recommended the abandonment of bee-houses altogether, I would say, place each hive upon a separate board supported by a single pedestal 4 or 5 inches in diameter—a piece of wood with the bark on does remarkably well; place it firmly in the ground, and about 15 inches from its surface. Upon the top of this post should be nailed firmly a piece of board 8 or 9 inches square, upon which should be placed the board the hive stands upon, but not united to it, so that the hive may be removed whenever required without disturbing the bees. Clay or mortar should never be used to fasten the hive to the board; the bees will do that in a much more effectual manner themselves, with a substance they collect from resinous trees, called propolis. Mortar or clay tends very much to decay the hives; and hives managed on this principle are expected to stand for fifteen or even twenty years. Let the hives be placed about 3 feet apart from each other, and in a right line.

Hives.—I am more and more convinced, from experience, that bees do much better in broad, shallow hives, than in any others. All the hives that I have used myself for the last three years, and those that I have had

1867] THE RECEIPT BOOK. 175

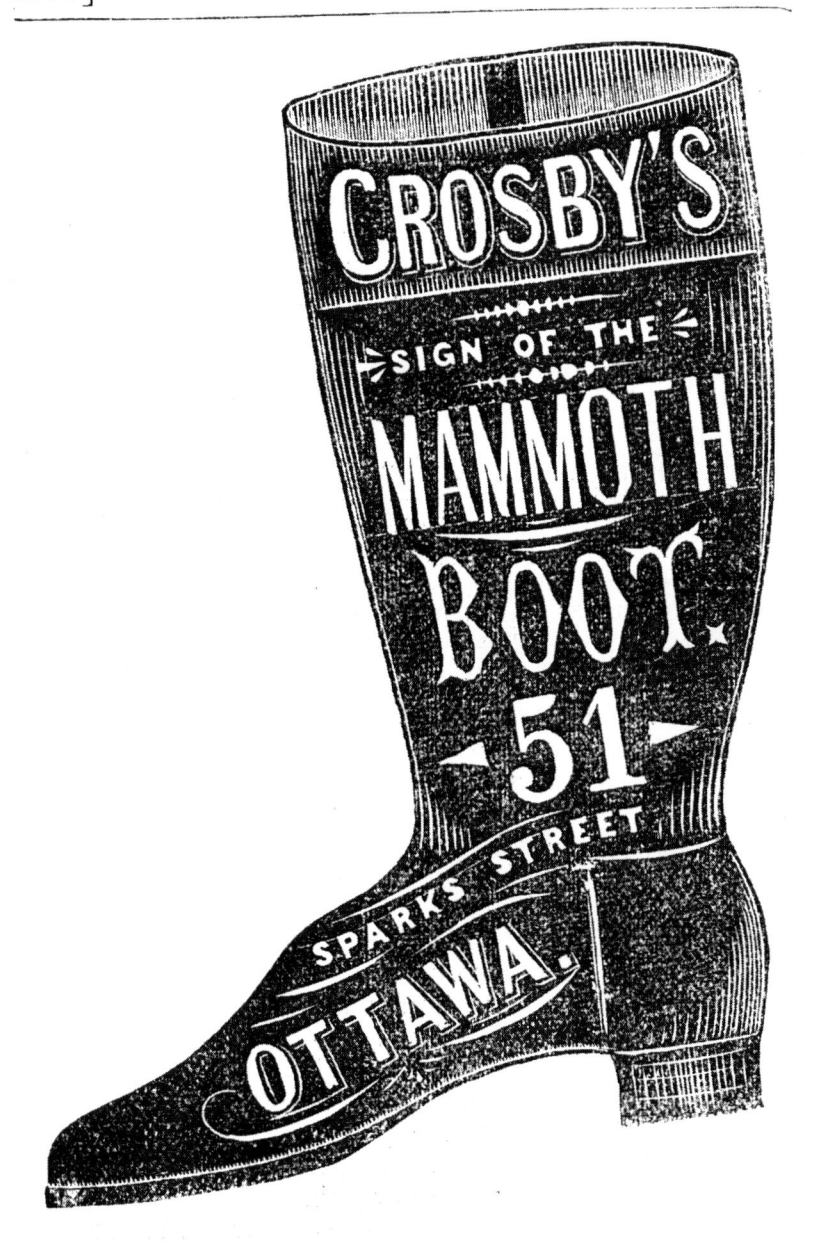

CROSBY'S
SIGN OF THE
MAMMOTH BOOT.
51
SPARKS STREET
OTTAWA.

made for the last two, have been of this kind—namely, 7 inches deep, and 14 inches wide, measuring in the inside. The only inconvenience that can possibly arise from a hive of this shape is, that from the great weight of supers which year after year it will have to bear, the top will sink a little; therefore, it should never be used without an adapting-board of 12 inches square; this will take the weight of the supers from the centre to the side of the hive.

Swarming.—Most people who have bees allow their swarms to remain till the evening in the place where they have alighted, and do not move them to the apiary till after sunset. This method has many inconveniences. As soon as a swarm has congregated in the new hive, and seems to be at ease in it, the most industrious among the bees fly off to the fields, but with a great many precautions; they descend the front of the hive, and turn to every side to examine it thoroughly, then take flight, and make some circles in the air in order to reconnoitre their new abode; they do the same in returning. If the swarm has taken flight in the morning the same bees make several excursions during the day, and each time with less precaution, as, becoming familiarised with their dwelling, they are less afraid of mistaking it: and thus, next morning, supposing themselves in the same place, they take wing without having observed were they have spent the night, and surprised at their return not to find the hive in the same place, they fly about all day in search of it, until they perish with fatigue and despair. Thus many hundreds of the most industrious labourers are lost; and this may be entirely avoided if the swarms be removed as soon as the bees are perceived coming out; this sign is alone sufficient. Experience has long since proved that the custom of beating warming-pans, and the like, at the time

Metropolitan Chop House,

Aumond's Block, Rideau Street, Ottawa,

P. O'MEARA, - - - PROPRIETOR.

This old established and favorite Chop-house will be found supplied with the Choicest Delicacies of the season. Hot Meals prepared at all hours, at the shortest notice. The best brands of Liquors and Cigars always on hand.

No trouble or expense is spared by the proprietor to maintain the reputation which this establishment has had of being a FIRST-CLASS HOUSE OF ENTERTAINMENT.

F. TRAUNWIESER,

MANUFACTURING

JEWELER,

14 ELGIN STREET,

Opposite the Post Office, OTTAWA.

MASONIC JEWELS MADE TO ORDER.

Every Description of Jewelry and Medals made to order, and neatly repaired at moderate charges.

For the Neatest and Cheapest

PRINTING,

GO TO

"The Ottawa Citizen."

OFFICE--RIDEAU STREET.

ALL ORDERS IN THE

BOOK-BINDING LINE

are executed in the most durable styles, at the lowest rates, and with promptness.

Special attention given to the manufacture of

BLANK BOOKS.

RULING DONE TO ANY PATTERN,

Neatly, Cheaply, and Promptly.

The Ottawa Citizen
STEAM PRINTING HOUSE!

Is replete with every requisite and appliance for the execution of

CHEAP, NEAT AND EXPEDITIOUS PRINTING,

Mammoth, Medium and Small Posters,
Hand Bills, Concert Bills, Railroad Bills, Show Bills.
Stage Bills, Steamboat Bills, Book, Magazines,
Cheque Books Business Cards, Professional Cards,
Funeral Cards,
Wedding Cards, Tickets, etc.,
Law Blanks, Municipal and Corporation Blanks,
Prommissory Note Books, etc.;
Printed in Black, Red, Blue, and other Colored Inks, and on White and Colored Paper.

BOOK-BINDING, BLANK BOOKS & PAPER RULING
IN EVERY STYLE.

CHEAPNESS, NEATNESS, and PUNCTUALITY are the Principal Features of the Establishment.

Orders sent by Mail Carefully and Promptly attended to, and Work despatched by Parcel Post without delay.

I. B. TAYLOR, Proprietor.

send out another swarm : this generally occurs in about a month, but it is a thing by no means to be desired, and should carefully be prevented by giving timely room.

Hiving.— Whatever system be adopted, let everything be in readiness for the reception of swarms; for even where the depriving system is followed, from some oversight on the part of the apiarian, a swarm will occasionally occur. Watch the swarm in silence, and after it has once collected, lose no time in housing it into a NEW, clean and dry hive (its weight, with the floor-board, being first taken and marked upon it), and let it be placed where it it is to remain within ten or fifteen minutes after the time of its being hived ; it will not be necessary even to wait till the bees clustered in front or on the sides of the hive are re-united to their companions insite, as they are never long in being so.

Hives with Comb in them.—Hives of comb, in which swarms of the last year have died, should be carefully preserved for hiving swarms into them ; it gives a swarm treated in this manner full three weeks advantage over another put at the same time into an empty hive.

Second Swarms.—A second swarm generally leaves the hive about nine days after the first ; but the time may be exactly ascertained by standing quietly beside the hive after sunset, when the queen may be distinctly heard, which is a certain indication that a second swarm will leave the hive. Should two or three queens be heard one after the other, it will be on the following day, if the whether be not very unfavorable. Should the queens continue to pipe after the departure of a second swarm, a third will certainly follow in a few days ; but if one or two queens be found dead beneath the

TRY

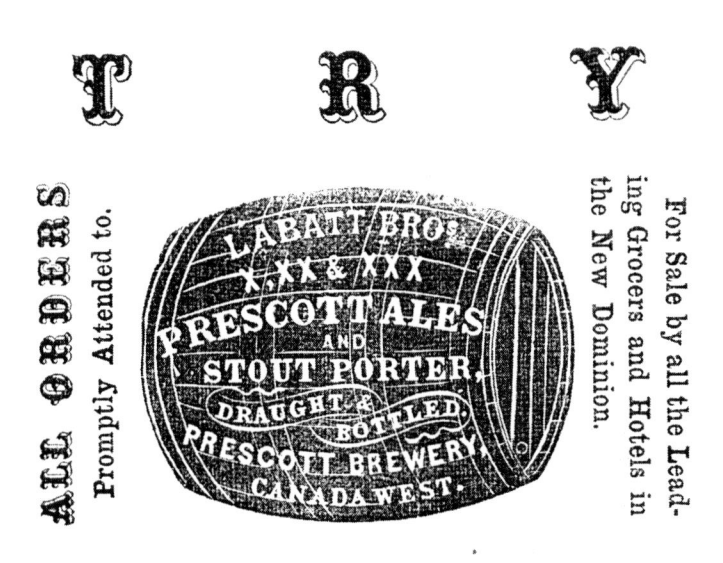

LABATT BROS
X, XX & XXX
PRESCOTT ALES
AND
STOUT PORTER,
DRAUGHT & BOTTLED,
PRESCOTT BREWERY,
CANADA WEST.

ALL ORDERS Promptly Attended to.

For Sale by all the Leading Grocers and Hotels in the New Dominion.

THOMAS DOWSLEY,

Wholesale Agent for Ottawa City.

hive on the next morning, no more swarms can be expected.

Uniting Swarms.—I must here observe that second and third swarms are very seldom, if ever, worth preserving by themselves; but two second swarms, when joined, are very little inferior in value to a first swarm, and the union is very easily effected in the following manner:—When two second swarms, or a second and third, come off on the same day, hive them separately, and leave them till an hour and a half after sunset; then spread a cloth upon the ground, upon which, by a smart and sudden movement, shake all the bees out of one of the hives, and immediately take the other and place it gently over the bees that are heaped together upon the cloth, wedging up one side about half an inch, that the bees outside may pass under, and they will instantly ascend into it and join those which, not having been disturbed, are quiet in their new abode. Next morning, before sunrise, remove this newly-united hive to the place in which it is to remain. This doubled population will work with doubled success, and in the most perfect harmony, and generally become a strong stock, from which much profit may be derived. Two second swarms, or a second and third, may be joined in the same manner, although one of them may have swarmed some days or even weeks later than the other; taking care, however, not to make the first one enter the second, but the second the first. A third and a fourth parcel of bees may be joined to them at different times in the same way till the stock becomes strong. It is impossible sufficiently to impress upon the mind of every one who keeps bees the necessity of having his stock ALL STRONG; for weak stocks are very troublesome, very expensive, and seldom, if ever, afford any profit. "The stronger the colony at the outset, the better the

OTTAWA

Cabinet Warehouse,

No. 1, RIDEAU STREET,

Near the Sapper's Bridge,

GEORGE SEALE, Agent.

A CHOICE COLLECTION OF ALL KINDS OF

FANCY AND DOMESTIC FURNITURE

KEPT CONSTANTLY ON HAND, OR

Made to Order with Despatch.

☞ DON'T FAIL TO INSPECT THE STOCK.

bees will work, and the more prosperous it will become. I never knew a weak one do well long; and a little extra expense at first is amply rewarded by succeeding years of prosperity and ultimate profit." And again, "Thus strength in one year begets it in succeeding ones; and this principle ought to be borne in mind by those who imagine that the deficient population of one season will be made up in the next, and that the loss of bees in the winter is of secondary consequence, forgetting how influential is their warmth to the earlier and increased productive powers of the queen; and how important it is, in the opening spring, to be able to spare from the home duties of the hive a number of collectors to add to the stores, which would otherwise not keep pace with the cravings of the rising generation. It is a remarkable fact, that two weak stocks joined will collect double the quantity of honey, and consume much less, than two of the same age and strength kept separately. Stocks must be joined after sunset, upon the day that one of them has swarmed; and the doubled stock must be placed upon the stand it previously occupied: great care must be taken not to shake the hive, nor must it be turned up. The combs, being new and tender, will easily break, and the stock by that means be destroyed.

Feeding.—The best kind of food that can be given to bees is honey liquefied with a small portion of warm water; but where honey is scarce and dear, an excellent substitute will be found in lump sugar. Three pounds of sugar to a pint of water, boiled for two or three minutes, and then mixed with a pound of honey, this will make five pounds of excellent food, which the bees appear to like quite as well as honey alone. An important circumstance connected with this subject has offered itself to my notice very recently—namely, that

"THE OTTAWA CITIZEN,"

PUBLISHED

DAILY & WEEKLY,

Is the Oldest Established and most Extensively Circulated Newspaper in the Ottawa Valley.

TERMS OF SUBSCRIPTION.

DAILY EDITION.—SIX DOLLARS a year when paid in advance; EIGHT DOLLARS a year when not paid in advance.

WEEKLY EDITION.—ONE DOLLAR a year when paid in advance; ONE DOLLAR and FIFTY CENTS when paid at any time during the current year; and TWO DOLLARS if not paid until the expiration of the year.

TERMS FOR ADVERTISING.

All Advertisements are measured by solid minion type, and are charged for at the following rates:

DAILY EDITION.—Eight Cents per line for the first insertion, and Two Cents a line for each subsequent insertion.

WEEKLY EDITION.—Ten Cents per line for the first insertion, and Four Cents per line for each subsequent insertion.

☞ No deviation whatever will be made from these rates for merely transient advertising; but merchants and other business men can contract on favorable terms, or Advertisements inserted, with or without changes of matter, by the year, half year or quarter. Professional Cards are inserted for $8 a year in each edition.

All announcements of Births, Marriages and Deaths are charged for as advertisements, at the rate of fifty cents each insertion, except in the case of Deaths accompanied with a notice of the funeral, when one dollar is charged.

of giving bees food in a solid state. By this means very great trouble and inconvenience will be avoided, both to the bees as well as to their proprietors; for the former will be in no danger of drowning, and will also have a supply of food that they appear to like better than any that has ever before been given to them; whilst the latter will be spared the trouble of preparing those compounds usually recommended, many of which I have always considered to be very injurious to the bees, and more especially so when given in large quantities in the autumn. After many experiments by myself and some apiarian friends, it is found that of all other solids barley-sugar has the decided preference with the bees. They will take it before anything else that is offered to them; and the rapidity with which they dissolve it is quite surprising. It may be given either at the top of a hive, where there is an opening, by tying half a dozen sticks together and covering them with a box or small hive, or even with a flower-pot, or at the bottom, as in the common straw hive, by pushing a few sticks in at the entrance, for, unlike liquid food, it does not attract robbers nor cause fighting, although given in the daytime. One of my friends supposes it to be the lemon flavor in the barley-sugar that is so pleasing to the bees; but to test the truth of this I had some made without lemon, and when both kinds were offered to them at the same time, the preference was given to the latter. I have tried the same also in liquid food; the lemon-flavoured is rejected for that without it. Another friend suggests it to be its deliquescent nature—that is, it becomes moist when exposed to the air, combined with its highly-purified state, which, in all probability, is the true reason, for here are no crystals to contend with, nor any disposition to form crystals, of which both loaf-sugar and sugar-candy consist; and even honey, when crystallised, is useless to the bees, and is cast out of the hive by them. It is certainly most convenient to be able to push a few sticks of barley-sugar under a weak hive, and to know that by so doing they are made secure from want for a time The idea of expense may be a consideration with some persons at first seeing barley-sugar recommended for this purpose ; but upon inquiry it will be found that it may be purchased for less than a shilling a pound, and it may be made for sixpence.

Manner of Taking Honey.—At noon, upon a clear fine day, pass either a very thin knife or fine wire between the hive and the glass intended to be taken. If this precaution be neglected, a piece of comb is frequently left projecting from the top of the one left, or the bottom of that taken, which will cause much trouble to the operator. Two adapting-boards placed between the hive and the glass will be found very convenient, for the knife or wire will then only have to be passed between them, and the danger of breaking the combs thus be obviated.

Stupifying Bees by Chloroform.—The necessary dose is a quarter of an ounce, or two teaspoonfuls, poured into a piece of rag doubled twice, and placed on the floor-board of the hive, which must be lifted up for the purpose, the entrance-hole being carefully secured. In about two minutes and a half there will be a loud humming, which lasts about one minute, when all is quiet. Let the hive remain in this state for six or seven minutes longer, making altogether about ten minutes. Remove the hive, and you will find the greater part of the bees lying senseless on the board. There will still be a few clinging between the combs, some of which may be brushed out with a feather. They return to animation in from half an hour to one hour after the operation. This plan, unlike the usual mode of brimstoning, and the more modern plan of fumigation by fungus or puff ball, is easily carried into operation, and the flavor of the honey is not injured by the fumes; but it is said to be highly injurious to the bees.

By Fumigation.—Much has been said and written upon the suject of fumigation, yet this is a process that I am not at all partial to; and, as far as my experience has gone, it is one which I have never yet had oocasion to resort to in a single instance; for even in the most difficult operations I have always found a puff, and yet a very little one, of tobacco-smoke to be all-sufficient. As I have said before, gentleness is the best protection; still, if by any little accident the bees become irritated, a slight puff of tobacco-smoke quiets them at once. One reason for my not being partial to fumigation is, that I could never see the necessity for it; and another reason is, that all the bees which I have seen thus treated are sluggish and inactive for some days after the operation, besides many having been killed. Now, this in early spring, or in the midst of the honey-gathering season is certainly of great consequence, especially when we are told that a prosperous colony of bees will, in a single day of the latter season, collect from 4 to 6 lbs. of honey.

Method of Draining Honey from the Combs.—Place a sieve, either of hair or canvass, over an earthen jar, cut the combs containing the honey into small pieces, and put them into a sieve; let them be cut in an horizontal direction. It is better to slice them twice—that is, at the top and bottom, than in the middle. Crushing or pressing should be avoided; for, as a portion of brood and bee-bread generally remains in the comb, pressure would force it through the sieve, and the honey would thereby be much injured, both in color as well as flavor. It is very desirable to have two sieves; for in every hive there will be two kinds or honey—the one almost colorless and fine-flavored, found at the side of the hive; the other dark and not so good, stored in the centre. These should always be kept separate. The draining process may occupy, perhaps, two days; but the largest quantity, as well as the best quality, will be drained off in three or four hours.

Preparation of Wax.—Having drained all the honey from the combs, wash these in clean water; this liquid, by exposure to the sun and air, will make most excellent vinegar; put them in a clean boiler with some soft water; simmer over a clear fire until the combs are melted: pour a quart or so into a canvass bag, wide at the top and tapering downwards into a jelly bag; hold this over a tub of cold water; the boiling liquor will immediately pass away, leaving the liquefied wax and the dross in the bag; have ready a piece of smooth board, of such a length that one end may rest at the bottom of the tub and the other end at its top; upon this inclined plane lay your reeking bag, but not so as to touch the cold water; then, by compressing the bag with any convenient roller, the wax will ooze through and run down the board into the cold water, on the surface of which it will set in thin flakes; empty the dross out of the bag and replenish it with the boiling wax, and proceed as before until all has been pressed. When finished, collect the wax from the surface of the cold water, put it into a clean saucepan with very little water, melt it carefully over a slow fire, skim off the dross as its rises, then pour it into moulds or shapes, and place them where they will cool slowly. The wax may be rendered still more pure by a second melting and moulding.

THE RECEIPT BOOK. [1867

O'CONNOR & WALLER,

EXCHANGE BROKERS,

Fire, Life and Accidental Insurance, Commission and

COLLECTING AGENTS.

OFFICE, No. 27 SUSSEX STREET.

COMPANIES REPRESENTED.

Hartford Live Stock Insurance Company,
CAPITAL $500,000

Queen Fire and Life Insurance Company,
CAPITAL $10,000,000

Phœnix Mutual Life Insurance Company,
CAPITAL $2,000,000

New York Casualty (Accidental) Ins. Co.,
CAPITAL $100,000

OLD
Aetna Insurance Company,
—OF—
HARTFORD, CONN.

Incorporated 1819. Charter Perpetual.

CASH CAPITAL, all paid up - $3,000,000
ASSETS at 1st July, 1867 - - - 4,650,938
LOSSES paid in 48 Years - - - 21,371,972

This Old and Favorite Company being NON-TARIFF, continues to insure, as HERETOFORE, at the lowest rates commensurate with the risks incurred.

Private Dwellings detached, their contents and Farm Property Insured for three years at greatly Reduced Rates.

For financial strength, liberal treatment of Policy Holders, and Promptness in the settlement of Losses,

THE ÆTNA OCCUPIES A FOREMOST POSITION.

☞ The large Assets of the Company have, within the last six months, been increased by a sum exceeding $400,000.

All Losses Paid Promptly in Canada Bankable Funds.

J. T. & W. PENNOCK, Agents,
SPARKS STREET, OTTAWA.

Index

A

apoplexy 72
apothecary 153
apples
  apple fool 24
  black cape 24
  dried 32
  marmalade 30
auctioneer/real estate agent 52

B

bad breath 60
bandoline 60
beans 14
bears grease 58
beef
  pickled beef 146
bees
  feeding 184
  fumigation 188
  hives 174
  hives with combs in them 180
  hiving 180
  manner of taking honey 187
  method of draining honey from the combs 188
  preparation of wax 188
  second swarms 180
  stupifying bees by chloroform 187
  swarming 176
  uniting swarms 182
beet-root 16, 18
berries
  preservation 150
bleaching liquor 56
book binders 89, 131
booksellers 157
brass foundry 139
bronchial tubes, worms on 72
bronzed lamps, to clean 66
butcher 141, 151
butternut
  pickled butternut 22

C

cabbage, red 14
cabinet-makers 99, 125, 183
cake
  biscuit cake 42
  cheap seed cake 40
  common bread cake 40
  gingerbread 44
  hard biscuits 44
  muffins 44
  observation on making and baking cakes 37
  plain and crisp biscuits 46
  plain bun 44
  pound cake 42
  sponge cake 42
  tea cakes 44
camphorated dentifice 58
candles, tallow 144
canning
  cement for canning fruits 150
carrots 18
cattle, diseases and remedies
  carget 78
  clue bound 78
  cow pox 72, 78
  diarrhea 78
  foul in the foot 80
  gut-tie 76
  hoove 78, 82
  hydrophobia 76
  inflammation of the bladder 82
  inflammation of the haw 82
  inflammation of the kidneys 84
  inflammation of the liver 84
  joint murrain 76
  lice 80
  mad staggers 74
  mange 80
  milk fever 74
  navel ill 84
  open joints 80
  pneumonia 74
  red water 74
  rheumatism 76
  rupture of the bladder 80
  thrush in the mouth 72, 76
  ulcers about the joints 72
  wood evil 82
  worms 72
  worms on the brain 80
  worms on the bronchial tubes 72
cauliflower 14
cement, cheap 158
cement, for china 156
cement, Russian 156
cement, waterproof, for clothing 158
chair covers, to clean 68
cherries
  dried without sugar 26
  dried with sugar 32
  preservation 150
china, cement for 156
china/glass, broken, to cement 66
cholera/diahrrea, remedy for 15
cider
  to refine cider 46
clothing 57
clue bound 78
coffee 63
collection agents 190
commission merchants 135
corns, cure for 72
cough emulsion 17
cucumbers 12
  pickled cucumbers 20
currants

black currant wine 48
jelly 30
preservation 36
preservation/to dry with sugar 152
wine 46

D

dentist/surgeon 143
domestic cookery 4
drugs/chemicals 49, 91, 103, 109, 115
dry goods/millinery 4, 7, 9, 35, 41, 43, 65, 73, 81, 113
dye
 black 50
 blue 50, 52
 cochineal scarlet 52
 dove and slate color 56
 fine wine color 52
 green 52
 lilac 56
 madder red 48
 pink 52
 salmon 56
 scarlet red 52
 yellow 52

E

eggs
 omlet 28

F

fabrics 79
flour 137
flummery 24
freckles 60
frost bite 72
fruit
 preservation for winter 34
 to candy 28
 to prepare for chicken 26

G

gas and steam fitting 52
ginger
 ginger wine 48
glassmaker 129
gold 85
gooseberries
 preservation 34
gooseberry
 jam 34
gooseberry fool 22
groceries 37, 75, 149

H

hairdress and perfumier 101
hair loss prevention 60
hair wash 60
hard soap with lard 140
hardware 39, 69, 119, 127
horse clothing 47
horses, diseases and remedies
 accidents 96
 broken wind 104
 colic 96
 corns 108
 difficulty in stalling 106
 distemper 102
 farcy 98
 fitts 93
 glanders 98
 inflammation of the skin of the heels 106
 jaundice 104
 lameness 94
 lampas 98
 overreach 108
 poll evil 100
 roaring 100
 saddle-galls 102
 spavin 102
 springhalt 106
 stabs or cuts 94
 strangles 100
 tendon strain 106
 thorough-pin 106
 windgalls 106
 worms 104

I

icing for cake 36
insurance 2, 190, 191
ironmonger 107

J

Japanned trays, to clean 66

K

kid gloves, to wash 68

L

lamps, chandeliers, and chimneys 61
leather goods 147
leather, hides and oils 117
lemons
 lemon marmalade 32
linen, to clean 66
liquid blueing 140
liquor 37
looking-glasses, to clean 66

M

macaroni 28
marrow and caster oil pomatum 58
mushroom 16, 18
 mushroom ketchup 22
music and fancy goods 77
mutton hams 148

N

navel ill 84

O

oil 93, 155
omlet 28
onions 12, 18
 pickled onions 20

oranges
  orange fool 24
  orange marmalade 32
Ottawa Citizen, The 185

P

papier mache, to clean 66
parsley 18
parsnips 18
peaches
  brandy 30
  preservation 148
pears
  baked pears 26
  preservation 148
  stewed pears 26
peas 12
photography 23, 25
pickles 18
pigs, diseases and remedies
  administering physic 110
  catarrh 110
  catching the pig 110
  crackings 112
  diarrhea 112
  fever 110
  foul skin 112
  heaving 110
  jaundice 114
  leprosy 114
  lethargy 114
  measles 116
  murrain 114
  points of a good hog 108
  quinsy 112
  sows with pigs 108
  spleen 112
  staggers 112
  surfiet 114
  tumors 114
plums
  little plum cakes 40
  plum cakes 36
  preservation 150
  preservation for winter pies 36

pomatum, common 58
pomatum, hard 58
pork
  pork preservation 148
poultry, diseases and remedies
  athsma 122
  costiveness 124
  diarrhea 126
  fattening 120
  fever 126
  indigestion 128
  lice 128
  loss of feathers 130
  pip 132
  poultry houses 122
  rearing of ducklings 118
  rearing of turkeys 118
  roup 134
  wounds and sores 136
preservation
  fruit for winter 34
  see also individual fruits and vegetables 16
  vegetables 16
printing 33, 178, 179
pudding
  baked apple 6
  baked rice 7
  batter 6
  batter with meat 6
  common pancake 10
  common plum 10
  custard 7
  lemon 6
  pancakes of rice 10
  plain rice 7
  suet 7
  Yorkshire 7

R

rabbit
  Welch rabbit 24
raspberries
  jam 34
  raspberry vinegar 40

raspberry wine 46
red cabbage
  pickled red cabbage 20
restaurants
  Metropolitan Chop House 177
rheumatism 76
rice
  buttered 20
  snow-balls 22

S

scouring liquor 56
sheep, diseases and remedies
  administering medicine 92
  apoplexy 90
  bleeding 92
  braxy 90
  bronchitis 90
  caked bag 86
  colic 90
  costiveness 88
  diarrhea 88
  feeling the pulse 92
  fouls 92
  fractures 88
  inflammation of the eyes 86
  maggot flies 86
  maggots 86
  palsy 86
  pelt rot 86
  snuffles 90
  sore face 88
  sore mouth 84
shoes/boots 11, 13, 59, 67, 97, 175
silk, black, to renovate 68
soap 144
soft soap 140
spinach 14
stains on cloth, removal
  fruit stains 64
  grease spots 64

ink stains 64
paint 64
wax spots 64
starching 68
strawberries
  preservation 150
  presevation 32
straw matting, to clean 66
suet 30
  preservation 30
syllabub 28

T

tailors 83, 173
tea 19, 21, 63
tinware, to mend 154
tobacco 123, 145
tomatoes
  preservation 150, 152
tooth wash 58

U

ulcers 72

upholstery 105

V

vegetables 10
  to boil green 10

W

wallpaper, to clean 66
washing fluid 138
watchmaker/jeweller 27, 31, 121, 133
watermelon
  preservation 152
water, to filter 154
weeds 156
wine
  black currant 48
  currant wine 46
  ginger 48
  raspberry wine 46
wine/spirits 29, 46, 63, 95, 181